My Chocolate Box Journey

Jim Dick

Acknowledgement

Grateful and sincere thanks to David and Jan Holdaway of *Life Publications* for their support and guidance throughout the whole process of publishing. Their professional expertise and spiritual input has been invaluable and their work has been the labour of friends not just publishers.

Holy Bible, New International Version® Anglicized, NIV® Copyright © 1979, 1984, 2011 by Biblica, Inc.® Used by permission. All rights reserved worldwide.

Contact

I can be contacted by email at: jimdick41@gmail.com
I would love to hear from you.

Life Publications
www.lifepublications.org.uk

Dedication

Margery and I would like to dedicate this book to the many friends who have been a part of our journey. Some made a brief appearance but left a lasting impression, while others have been with us for a large part of our journey and continue to bless our lives. It has been said that, 'the most valuable antique is a dear old friend'. Our grateful thanks to every one of our 'dear old (and young) friends'; they laughed with us in our happy times and they wept with us in our sad times. They were, and still are, true friends and we thank God for every one of them.

Commendations

This is a remarkable book written by a much loved and respected Christian leader who has been a pastor, Bible College Principal, national leader and respected author. We often act as though Christian leaders live on a different plane, untouched by the challenges that face others. Jim Dick explodes that myth telling the story of the 'journey' of his life through times of triumph and trauma. His story will inspire you to trust and draw from God through the seasons of your own life.

Chris Cartwright
General Superintendent Elim Church

My first official act as the Regional Leader for Scotland was to induct Jim and Margery Dick into the Kilsyth Church of God. During those following days, Jim and Margery knew the best of times and the worst of times. In your hand, you have the opportunity to read something truly amazing from two awesome people. This book is inspirational as they share their journey, with integrity and honesty. Be ready to be inspired!

Kevin Peat
Regional Leader, Elim Churches in Scotland and NW England

My wife Jan and I have been privileged to know Jim and Margery for over thirty years. Their friendship and ministry have blessed and enriched our lives as well as so many others. Jim's *Chocolate Box Journey* through their green pastures and dark valleys of life will stir your faith and deeply move your heart. It's an amazing story of God's faithfulness, comfort, love and victory. Read and be blessed.

David Holdaway
Principal of the Bible College of Wales

Contents

My Chocolate Box Journey

Foreword

I have heard over many years the same phrase used by many, many people, especially Elim Ministers; 'I really appreciate Jim and Margery Dick!'

Over the years Jim has held some of the highest positions within the Elim Pentecostal Church and many people either know of him or in fact know him well, and this knowledge has brought this response of love and appreciation.

However, the story of his life and service may not be fully known in depth by all, in fact much of the private and personal world of Jim Dick may never have been fully explored, until now.

The journey of his life and that of Margery his wife has had many high and wonderful moments contrasting with many dark and troubled valleys. Jim lays it all open in this 'life story' and it portrays a man who is fully committed to God's plan for his life. The story also constantly shows the amazing grace of God in a life that is dedicated to Christian service.

Carole and I have known Jim for almost half a century and I have worked alongside him and travelled with him on many occasions. We have preached together, laughed together and shared many low times too. We have ministered together on committees and in Leadership Seminars as well as serving for many years on Elim's National Executive Council and National Leadership Team, so I know him extremely well. But I discovered more about him while reading through 'his chocolate box story' and have come to love and appreciate him and Margery even more.

Jim unpacks his story in a very candid way and is transparent and honest about his journey, recalling 'the good, the bad, and the ugly' in a forthright way that carries the reader along, almost as if we are looking over his shoulder as the journey unfolds. I commend this book which should be read by people of faith or people of no faith.

I am very privileged to be asked to write this Foreword and I thank God for a 'life time' friend called Jim. I also know that the whole of the Elim Pentecostal Church thank God, too, for Jim Dick, the Man of God, who has served so faithfully and so well. This is his story!

Geoff Feasey
Former Elim Regional Superintendent

Introduction

You may be wondering about the title of this book, *My Chocolate Box Journey*. I heard it used in the film *Forrest Gump* which is the story of a boy born with leg problems and forced to wear callipers but who later discovered that he could run, and very fast. It is a story of one young man's battle with his problems and how he triumphed over them. In the film Forrest refers to the words of his mother on the subject of life – *'life is like a box of chocolates; you never know what you're going to get'*. And by that she meant there will be some 'bites' on the journey of life that are very nice, other bites that may not be our first choice but they are all part of the chocolate box of life.

I have called this book *My Chocolate Box Journey* but really it should be *'Our' Chocolate Box Journey* because it is as much about Margery as me. She has been my wonderful companion on this journey for fifty three years of our marriage and I could never have made the journey without her. She is my 'wonder woman' of Proverbs 31 – an amazing wife, mother, home-maker, counsellor, leader's wife plus a host of other attributes. Having her by my side for life's adventure has been one of God's greatest gifts to me and I constantly thank Him for her. Proverbs 12:4 says, *'A wife of noble character is her husband's crown.'* Well put by Solomon. By the way we both have a weakness for chocolate so the title is appropriate.

Every person has a life story and each one is personal and unique. In this book I want to share with you some of the variety that has been in my 'chocolate box journey'. It has had some lovely tasting parts, some not so nice and a few that I did not enjoy at all. I will try to give you a snapshot of some of the events that have helped shape my life and maybe when you see the extraordinary grace of God in a very ordinary life it will help you on your journey. In fifty years in ministry I have had a fantastic journey, been to some wonderful places and met some quite extraordinary people. I will enjoy introducing you to some of them. On my journey I have had some great experiences and learned quite a few things and I hope that some of this life wisdom will help make a contribution for the journey of your life.

Losing Dignity and Discovering Destiny

She wasn't very tall but the tone of voice indicated she was used to being obeyed. 'Take all your clothes off except for your socks and shoes and put this gown on'. Before you jump to some wrong conclusions I was in Stonehouse Hospital for an X-ray, so I had no choice but to obey the nurse who was speaking to me but I was a bit nervous about what might happen next. Unfortunately the gown I had been given was designed for someone considerably smaller than I was and you would need to have been a contortionist to reach the ties at the back (why do they put them there?). The gown didn't meet at the back and the dressing gown didn't meet at the front and both stopped at my knees and with socks and shoes sticking out at the bottom I looked a ridiculous sight!

Introduction

The curtain was soon pulled back and the same nurse issued another command, 'Follow me'! I could have wished for a secret passage to get to the X-ray department but that wasn't to be, she led me right through the middle of Outpatients, which, of course, was crowded. What a spectacle, the Reverend James Hawkins Dick trying to keep up with the nurse and maintain some sadly lacking dignity. I could not look to the right or the left but was convinced that the place was full of people who knew me well. After the X-ray the same nurse did a reverse procedure on me (back through Outpatients of course) and by the time I got back to the cubicle I was grateful to get dressed and escape back to normal life. I needed healing of the memories!

The event at the hospital was still on my mind as later that day I arrived at a meeting for some Pentecostal pastors. As I walked into the room my friend Peter Cochrane, the Scottish Assemblies of God Regional Superintendent was busy recounting something he felt God had told him recently and as I walked in the door these were the words he was repeating that God had said, 'Lose your dignity and discover your destiny'. The words hit me like a revelation and suddenly the recent event became like a parable that I was the main character in.

We humans (and especially men) have gained a lot of expertise in the art of covering ourselves up so that people don't see what's really going on inside us. We can hide behind our titles, a smoke screen of busyness, isolation, secrecy etc. I suppose the first 'cover up' happened in the Garden of Eden when Adam and Eve became aware of their nakedness and sewed leaves together.

God's ways for us can be hard to accept but in the end they work and for us to gain or make progress sometimes there has to be a willingness to lose and let go of some 'fig leaves', which we use to cover up our embarrassment, nakedness or inadequacies.

The pre-conversion Apostle Paul was a very proud man who certainly knew what his mission in life was and it was pursued with confidence and force; until he met Jesus and was knocked off his (high) horse. He was then taken on a journey of massive personal change and eventually he declared that for *'the sake of Christ he had suffered the loss of all things'* but also that he had come to realise they really only were 'manure'. After his encounter with Christ he began to look on life with different eyes and could later declare that *'the things that have happened to me have served to advance the gospel'*. This included 'things' that were unpleasant, costly and sometimes life threatening, but he chose to see them as events that God had used to cut a clearing through the obstacles of life for others to benefit from.

In this book I want to share with you some of my personal journey throughout my life but especially over the last few years which have been life changing.

There have been some significant 'losses', which actually turned out to be stepping-stones to 'gains'. No one has control over what happens to them in life but we do have control over what we do with what happens to us in life. How we respond can make them stumbling blocks or stepping-stones, making us bitter or better.

Introduction

Steve Covey in his book *The 7 Habits of Highly Successful People* states that, to him, the four main purposes of life are; to live, love, learn and leave a legacy. I have been privileged to experience the first three and hope that this book will play a small part in the fourth.

It amazes me that this book is in print; it amazes me even more that you have started to read it (I hope you will continue). I have been incredibility blessed throughout my life but the recent years have been the most challenging, very educational and hopefully the most productive.

I can tell you the moment that the season of my life changed dramatically; it was 7:40am on the morning of Monday February 7, 1998. The phone rang, it was Margery and it wasn't her usual tone of voice. Margery had gone down to Bristol to care for our daughter, Lorraine, who had been very unwell since coming back from Bangladesh.

Some background is necessary here: Lorraine was a nurse who after several years of having a great time in nursing and backpacking round the world had decided that it was time for her to try and use her nursing skills to 'make a difference'. She had signed up to work with VSO (Voluntary Service Overseas) and they had sent her to Bangladesh to help in training local nurses. We were very proud of her and kept in touch regularly. She had unexpectedly returned from Bangladesh and when she finally got to us in Scotland we were shocked at her emaciated condition. The doctor had diagnosed an *e-coli* type infection. Margery soon put her own nursing skills to work and after a lot of tender loving care Lorraine got back to more like her usual self and felt well enough to go back to Bristol to take up nursing again.

All seemed well for a while but a call from Lorraine had Margery travelling down to Bristol to care for her once more. But now back to the early morning phone call; Margery began to tell me that Lorraine was indeed unwell but not in the way we had thought, Margery had finally discovered the awful truth, Lorraine was a heroin addict. So, for Margery and I, and our whole family began the frightening and very dark journey which must be every parent's nightmare; I will share more of this part of the journey later in the book

On any interesting journey it is good to stop occasionally and take stock of where you are, where you've come from and where you are going. As I write this I have passed the milestone of becoming 70 and feel quite shocked that it has sneaked up on me and arrived before I felt ready for it. But it has caused me to pause, look back and draw lessons from the journey thus far and use the wisdom (hopefully) gained to better prepare for the important and hopefully exciting part that is still ahead.

On any journey it is important to make sure you set out with the right equipment, so in the next chapter I will focus on the importance of going to the right source to find wisdom for living a good life. As Christians, we do not believe in reincarnation so because we only get one shot at life, it is important we get the best information on how to live it well. The good news is that this information is freely available for all who want it so before I begin the story of my journey let us look at the wisdom that is available from God's Word for all of us.

Living Well

I was raised not too many miles from Blantyre, the birthplace of David Livingstone and as a young man I visited the memorial to his life which is situated in the actual building where he was born. His life and mission challenged me.

He was born in 1813 into a home where his father used to read him stories of great missionary exploits. One day David Livingstone got to his knees and said this prayer, 'Lord, send me anywhere, only go with me. Lay any burden on me, only sustain me. Sever any ties, but the ties that bind me to your service and to your heart,' and the Scripture came to him, *'Lo, I am with you always, even to the very end of the age.'*

After theological training and medical school Livingstone travelled to Africa. Biographical accounts tell us that when he walked into any university on his rare return visits home, students and faculty would rise to a standing ovation because they knew they were standing in the presence of a giant of a man. With his worn appearance through being almost blinded in one eye after being hit by a tree branch, his skin burnt brown by the African sun and an arm damaged as a result of being attacked by a lion, he told them what sustained him through all his travels and trials was God's presence and promise that He would never leave him or forsake him.

He was a missionary and explorer who opened up a way for modern missions to Africa that is now seeing countless thousands come to Christ. Reinhard Bonnke followed as a missionary to Africa years later and told how in 1985 he had ministered in Blantyre, Malawi, named after Livingstone's home town. Bonnke saw thousands responding to the Gospel in that mission. While there one of his co-workers was reading Livingstone's account of his time there that said, 'The work is hard, the Africans come to Christ in ones and twos, but one day they will come in their thousands.'

After years in Africa Livingstone's body began to give way. One day, preaching from a stretcher, literally trembling, he looked at two of his African brothers and said, 'Please take me back home. I am very, very ill. I'm very tired, I need some sleep.'

In the morning of May 1, 1873, his companions found him kneeling – he died while in prayer. His embalmed body was carried overland by his loyal attendants to be brought to Britain while his heart was buried in his beloved Africa. He was entombed in Westminster Abbey where his epitaph includes the words:

'Brought by faithful hands over land and sea here lies David Livingstone, missionary, traveller, philanthropist. For 30 years, his life was spent in an unwearied effort to evangelize the native races, to explore the undiscovered secrets, to abolish the desolating slave trade of Central Africa.'

His memorial is in one of the greatest buildings in the land but he died exactly the way he had lived – in the presence of his Lord.

David Livingstone ran well and finished well for God. What a tragedy to get to the end of life and find you have been cheated, that all you planned for, strived for and worked for turned out to be hollow, worthless and insubstantial. How sad that many will discover too late, that there was a far better way to have lived and that they missed out on the real life because no one gave them the wisdom to know how to live life well. The good news is that wisdom from the very best and most reliable source is freely available to all who really want it.

When the Queen of Sheba came to visit Solomon she came because she had heard of his amazing wisdom, but when she arrived in Jerusalem she not only heard his wisdom, she also 'saw' his wisdom. She saw this in the amazing life-style of Solomon and his people. True wisdom leads to an observable and measurable lifestyle that works and brings satisfaction. At the beginning of his long reign God made Solomon an amazing offer – *'ask for whatever you want'*. He asked for wisdom and understanding in order to live and reign wisely and God was so pleased with his choice of wisdom that he 'threw in' all the other things Solomon could have asked for but didn't.

For Solomon, at the beginning of his long reign as King, wisdom was the chief thing. Later, when he was instructing his own son on how to live well he reflected on his time as a boy – *'when I was a boy in my father's house...he taught me...get wisdom...wisdom is supreme'*. The Book of Proverbs was written by Solomon as a gift to his son to help prepare him for the challenges of life. A quote from Eugene Peterson's paraphrase of the Bible, *The Message*, and his introduction to the Book of Proverbs is worth reading:

'Many people think that what's written in the Bible has mostly to do with getting people into heaven – getting right with God, saving their eternal souls. It does have to do with that, of course, but not mostly. It is equally concerned with living on this earth – living well, living in robust sanity. In our Scriptures heaven is not the primary concern, to which earth is

17

a tag-a-long afterthought. "On earth as it is in heaven" is Jesus' prayer.

'"Wisdom" is the biblical term for this "on-earth-as-it-is-in-heaven" everyday living. Wisdom is the art of living skilfully in whatever conditions we find ourselves. It has virtually nothing to do with information as such, with knowledge as such. A college degree has no certification of wisdom – nor is it primarily concerned with keeping us out of moral mud puddles, although it does have a profound moral effect upon us.

'Wisdom has to do with becoming skilful in honouring our parents and raising our children, handling our money and conducting our sexual lives, going to work and exercising leadership, using words well and treating our friends kindly, eating and drinking healthily, cultivating emotions within ourselves and attitudes towards others that make for peace. Threaded through all these items is the insistence that the way we think of and respond to God is the most practical thing we do. In matters of everyday practicality, nothing, absolutely nothing, takes precedence over God.'

For 21st century Christians, with the benefit of New Testament revelation, we now know that *'in Christ are hidden all the treasures of wisdom and understanding'*, so for people today getting to know Christ and developing a consistent walk with Him opens the door to a wonderful treasure house of wisdom and understanding to enable us to live life well, the life that Jesus Himself described as *'life in all its fullness'*.

If wisdom for life is the chief thing, not power, money, success, position or promotion, then getting started on this journey of discovery is vital so, where do we begin? The answer may surprise you: **'The fear of the Lord is the beginning of wisdom.'**

'The fear of the Lord is the beginning of wisdom and knowledge of the Holy One is understanding,' Proverbs 9:10. Or as *The Message* paraphrases it, *'Skilled living gets its start in the Fear-of-God, insight into life from knowing a Holy God.'*

Most people want deliverance from fear but this is one fear that is beneficial and healthy. The book of Job has some remarkable insights and word pictures, and for those from a mining background chapter 28 will hold a special fascination. It draws the picture of ancient miners tunnelling deep into the earth in search of precious metals and stones but, says Job, no matter how deep you tunnel in the earth or how deep you go down into the sea you will not find wisdom in the depths. He asks the question, *'where is it to be found?'* The answer is that God alone knows the way to wisdom, He alone knows where it is to be found and He has shared the secret with those who earnestly seek it, *'The fear of the Lord - that is wisdom, and to shun evil is understanding,'* Job 28:28.

'The remarkable thing about fearing God,' says Oswald Chambers, 'is that when you fear God you fear nothing else but when you don't fear God you fear everything else.'

The question must therefore be asked 'if the fear of God is the beginning of wisdom, especially wisdom for living a good life, why is it that so few know anything about the fear of the Lord?' Surely understanding the importance of living with a sense of holy awe and reverence and being motivated by a loving fear of doing anything that would or could offend God should therefore be the highest priority of life? In an age of information overload and options mayhem as well as knowledge explosion, wisdom is in short supply – especially the practical kind to help us live life well. We are knowledge rich and wisdom poor. Wisdom is more than important it is crucial and as I said at the beginning of this chapter, it is too late to get to the end of your life and find out you took the wrong road, finding you failed to work for the really important things in life like healthy, loving and lasting relationships and not for a series of short term ones and one night stands. Also, the tragedy of discovering you accumulated a lot of money but never really used it to lasting and eternal benefit and had after all to leave it behind.

A holy, loving, reverential and awe inspired fear of God will affect how we live our lives; it will affect how we treat people and will provoke us to reject the self-obsessed and hedonistic culture of today.

Today, too many Christians hunger after blessing, personal destiny insights, prosperity and happiness, almost anything but the most important thing – walking in the fear of the Lord which is the beginning of wisdom. The fear of the Lord is not discovered by mistake or chance, it is a benefit that comes by diligently seeking and actively pursuing it.

In my recent readings of the Bible I have been impressed by some of its characters who took important journeys into fear, the fear of the Lord, and the lasting effect it had on their lives. Most today want to journey out of and away from fear and yes, there are many fears we need to get rid of, but the fear of the Lord is not one of them.

David's journey into fear

At the age of thirty David came into a marvellous season of prosperity and success. After almost a decade and a half of uncertainty, pressure, running, fear and being misjudged and maligned, suddenly in a very short space of time God united and established the Kingdom of Israel under his control. From a life of being a fugitive and constantly on the run and living in caves he found himself living securely with his family in a palace, surrounded by his mighty men, the whole nation united under his rule and all his enemies subdued. It must have been a marvellously euphoric experience.

But in the midst of his new found peace and security a new passion began to grip the heart of David, he wanted to bring the Ark of the Covenant, which symbolised the very presence of God, back into the centre of the nation's life in the newly captured Jerusalem. Despite all he now had the absence of 'The Presence' in the capital of the nation diluted all the other blessings. This now became his grand passion. After years of the nation neglecting and ignoring the Ark of the Covenant, David's first task was to discover where the Ark had been for all those years of abandonment.

After a diligent search he found the Ark and then set about calling the nation together to join him in the great spiritual task of bringing it to Jerusalem; this he achieved in a spectacular way so much so that the day the Ark was brought back saw the largest gathering of people the nation had ever seen. It wasn't just the size of the crowd it was also the passion and enthusiasm of the people. David's own passion had infected everyone present and it was an occasion motivated by a recently united nation's determination to please God.

The scene was one of high emotion with David out in front leading the people in joyful praise to God surrounded by thirty thousand chosen men and a whole nation who had come from every part of the Kingdom. It was an event overflowing with sincerity and joy. The Ark of God's presence was coming to Zion and into the centre of national life in the midst of wonderful music, choirs, singing, dancers and percussionists. Even as I write I can feel something of the overwhelming sense of joy at this event. No one could remember such a joyful national occasion and for David nothing was more important at the start of his reign.

The journey from the house of Abinadab where the Ark had resided for many years was going well. The cart carrying the Ark was a new one and Abinadab's sons, Uzzah and Ahio, were guiding the oxen and watching over the Ark; suddenly the oxen stumbled and it looked as though the Ark was in danger of falling off the cart. Uzzah reached out his hand to steady the Ark.

But then it happened! God struck Uzzah dead and the whole massive, joyful and exciting occasion came to an abrupt and unceremonious halt. God was angry. With such an obviously right project and with such deep sincerity, not only from David but also from the whole nation, how could God break into the event in such a dramatic and decisive way? How could God be so angry with a people who were so intent on pleasing him?

What a lesson for us today. The size of the crowd, the sincerity of the purpose, the care taken in the planning, the volume and skill of the musicians, the excitement of all present does not guarantee that God will always be pleased. David was undoubtedly doing the right thing but in the midst of his enthusiasm and excitement he had missed a vital ingredient in the great task of seeing God's presence restored back into the midst of God's people.

The account of this sobering event in 1 Samuel states that Uzzah was guilty of an irreverent act. It wasn't just what he did but what was going on in his heart as he did it. This young man had grown up with the Ark of God in his house; maybe such close proximity to 'The Presence' had developed a carelessness and familiarity in him. This event on the road up to Zion would certainly produce a renewed appreciation of the fear of God.

David was angry with God that day. His attempt to honour the Lord had resulted in an unprecedented display of God's wrath and in front of the whole nation. What a start to the beginning of his reign over the newly united nation. The place where it happened was given a new name – Perez Uzzah (outbreak against Uzzah) and forever after that name was a memorial to the whole nation of an unprecedented display of God's wrath.

Soon David's anger changed to fear, however, and that day David was introduced to an understanding of God that he'd never had before. There was an 'otherness' to God that was a new lesson. It was the beginning of a new wisdom for David and the start of a three month spiritual search to find out where he had gone wrong because he realised that as leader it was his responsibility to make sure the lesson served a purpose and was not pointless and unproductive.

Very carefully the Ark was carried aside into the house of Obed Edom, the whole nation went back to their homes bewildered and saddened and David began his spiritual post mortem examination. During the three month period of reflection David came to realise that sincerity, dedication, passion, enthusiasm, and a highly charged emotional event were not enough. It wasn't enough just to do the right thing it had to be done in the right way (the prescribed way) – God looks at every detail and not just at a good intention. David's journey into the fear of the Lord was also one into the beginning of a new wisdom.

Sadly the word 'awesome' has been trivialised and devalued by inappropriate and casual use and is easily applied to anything exceptionally good, even a meal on a plate will be described as 'awesome'. The proper use of the word however should be reserved for 'God' occasions. Only people who know something of the awesome, overwhelming and emotionally draining presence of God will be fit to make an impact on this money and experience obsessed generation. We have a need to rediscover the fear of the Lord to know how to live effectively in this the final age.

Maybe, like David, you have embarked on a worthy project for God and His glory and like David you have seen it crumble to failure in front of your eyes and you are asking the question 'why Lord, what did I do wrong?' Maybe you feel angry, disappointed and very confused about what you need to do to please God and find His favour. Could I encourage you to follow David's example and press through the anger into a quest to find the deeper purposes of God and the better way of doing the obviously right thing (the prescribed way)?

Referring again to Job's quest for wisdom for life and the fact that it was not to be found in the depths of the sea or the depths of the earth, 'where shall wisdom be found?' was his question and Job discovered that it was not to be found in the pious platitudes and well-worn clichés of the pseudo wisdom of his alleged friends. As Warren Wiersbe states in his commentary on Job, 'The three men had knowledge but they lacked wisdom'. To be sure, declares Job, you need to dig deep to find wisdom but make sure you dig in the right place. Miners risk their lives for the reward of gold and precious metals, surely, for God's people, some effort and risk is warranted to find the greatest treasure – wisdom to live our one life well. God is vitally concerned about people finding wisdom for a good life and so He has made available to us the wisdom of His Word and His Son.

Warren Wiersbe asks and answers the question 'What is "the fear of the Lord"? It is loving reverence for God, who He is, what He says and what He does (Malachi 2:5, 6). It is not a fear that paralyses, but one that energizes. When you fear the Lord, you obey His commands (Ecclesiastes 12:13), walk in His ways (Deuteronomy 8:6), and serve Him (Joshua 24:14). You are loyal to Him and give Him wholehearted service (2 Chronicles 19:9). Like Job, when you fear the Lord you depart from evil (Proverbs 3:7-8). The "fear of the Lord" is the fear that conquers fear (Psalm 112); for if you fear God you need not fear anyone else (Matthew 10:26-31).'

'Life is for living' the TV advert tells us, and real success is to live life well and to do this the journey commences by developing a right relationship with God which starts with a holy, reverential and loving awe of an almighty God.

The Christian life is likened to a journey; in fact the original title for believers in the New Testament was *'people of the Way'*. The title 'Christian' (belonging to Christ) was given by non-believers and was probably used as an insult, but originally they were people of *'the Way'* and so to be a follower of Christ meant you had obeyed an invitation to 'follow Him' and start on a journey of discovery.

1

The Start of the Journey

The target for the German Luftwaffe on the night of May 5, 1941 was Clydebank. My brother Tom, who was 18 and would shortly be leaving home to 'join up', was on warden duty at the time so he was able to tell all the neighbours that Bessie Dick had been blessed with a son, 'James'. It had come as a complete surprise to most and more of a shock to my mother and father that I was 'on-the-way', especially due to the fact that my brother was 18, my sister, Ina, was 15, my mother was in her forties and she was caring for her aged parents in her home and they were in need of a lot of attention.

All of this in 42 Toll Street (our home) which was a one bed-roomed house with an inside toilet but no bathroom, and there was a war on. The idea of a new baby into this already overcrowded accommodation and in the midst of severe war-time economic restrictions was one that caused doubts to my mother about her ability to cope with it all. My grandmother was aware of my mother's fears and being a woman of known prophetic foresight reassured my mother with the confidence that the baby would be a boy and that he would be a blessing and support in her later years. So on the night of May 5 James Hawkins Dick made his grand entrance into the world in the midst of a German air raid taking the total up to seven people living in the room and kitchen accommodation.

My father, also James, worked as an engineer in what was then known as Colville's steel works, later known as Ravenscraig. My mother and father were committed members of South Dalziel Parish Church where my father was one of a board of 45 elders. Life for my family by the standards of the day was good albeit a bit crowded. We were not affluent but there was sufficient for all the daily needs and the income allowed for the once-a-year July fair fortnight family holiday at Rothesay – the Scottish West Coast Riviera.

The 'doon-the-water' excursion found us boarding in the front room of the Morrison family home and enjoying regular trips on the renowned Clyde steamers with quaint names like Jeanie Deans, Talisman, Duchess of Montrose, Caledonia and Waverley, taking us to exotic sounding places like the Kyle's of Bute, Arrochar and Tighnabruaich. In the days before cheap international travel and package holidays the Clyde resorts were crowded with Scottish holiday makers, often enduring very un-summer-like but typical Scottish weather. Those two week holidays were a very far cry from today's 'long-haul' holidays to far off places but for me the island of Bute was my far flung place and Port Bannatyne and Ettrick Bay were my exotic places meriting extensive exploration.

In my childhood days there was a programme on the radio called *Friday Night is Music Night*, well for me Friday night was bath night and no matter who came to the home the zinc bath was hauled in, filled with hot water and placed in front of the fire. The clothes horse was then place around it to protect some of my boyish modesty and I was subjected to what I was instructed is next to godliness!

The house may have been crowded but it was a happy home, however, when I turned eleven my family's life changed dramatically with the discovery that my father had throat cancer (he was a pipe smoker). In those days before our now well-developed financial support network, not working meant no income and so by the age of twelve I had three 'out of school time' jobs to supplement the family's much depleted income. It was during this long and eventually terminal illness that there was another major event that profoundly affected the rest of my life. It started with my grandfather remarrying, an event which caused some serious disturbance in the wider family. The lady my grandfather married, however, was an unmistakable provision from God.

Aunt Helen, as she came to be known, was a born-again Christian and her influence and invitations resulted in the conversion of me, my mother, my father and my sister. It was in 1953 that a young and very fiery evangelist by the name of Alex Tee hit Motherwell like a tornado. His very forthright 'foursquare' gospel message of Christ as Saviour, Healer, Baptiser and Coming King caused serious disturbance in the very staunchly conservative church fraternity. Many of the local churches lost key members to the new and rapidly growing Elim Church but it was in July of 1952 that Alex Tee invited Duncan Campbell to Motherwell for a two week tent mission in Merry Street. Mr Campbell had been mightily used by God in the revival in the Hebrides and arrived in Motherwell from the Isle of Lewis with the fire of revival still burning in his soul and in his sermons.

It was my grandfather's new wife who found out about the mission and invited us along to hear the message of salvation and healing. Although I was only 12 years of age I well remember the night I was converted. It was marked by a deep sense of conviction and the sobbing I experienced continued for a long time after the meeting ended.

After the meeting Mr Campbell prayed with me in a small side tent and introduced me to the wonderful promise of John 10:27, 28 – *'my sheep listen to my voice; I know them, and they follow me. I give them eternal life, and they shall never perish, no-one can snatch them out of my hand.'* Shortly after this life-changing event my mother and I were baptised by Alex Tee at a service in the Motherwell public swimming pool. My mother and I were the first people Alex ever baptised; previously this had always been done by his father Harry Tee, past President of the Kilsyth Westport Hall (now known as the Kilsyth Church of God).

Our home at 42 Toll Street was very close to the church building in Airbles Road and so was frequently used to entertain special guest speakers. One such guest was Congo missionary Jimmy Salter. In the church service he had recounted some amazing experiences he and fellow missionary Willie Burton had had during the Congo revival and after the meeting, around the supper table in our home, he asked me what I wanted to be when I grew up. Well, who wants to be an engineer or drive a train when you have been listening to the miracle adventures of a real live apostle? 'I want to be a missionary,' was my reply. The answer he gave to my father startled me but nevertheless lodged in my mind and spirit, 'Mr Dick, don't allow this boy to go into the ministry until he's served his time in the steel works.' My father, who by this time could not speak because of the cancer, wrote on his pad, 'Jim, never forget that good advice.' It wasn't the answer I expected but it was the answer I needed.

Shortly after this my father died from his throat cancer. His illness had been very traumatic and for me it was an emotional and formative experience to watch his quiet endurance during a lot of suffering. My father's experience of God's grace was very quiet and private, in keeping with the kind of man he was. For my mother, now a widow, life in 1953 was not easy for her since there was little or no financial help from the state so for me the three jobs before and after school continued.

I left school at 15 and remembering the advice of Jimmy Salter went to an engineering college for a year's pre-apprenticeship training course. When this was completed I started an engineering apprenticeship in a boiler making company called Marshall and Anderson and finally ended up as a draughtsman. By this time I had come to realise that there was a call of God on my life for the full-time ministry, but I determined to finish my training in engineering before considering Bible College.

Time spent in the real world is still essential training for anyone considering the ministry. After all, the Lord Himself spent thirty years in the university of life before He entered His three years of public ministry and many of those thirty years were spent as an apprentice carpenter and finally as a qualified journeyman working to support His family after the death of Joseph.

It was during these 'silent' years, when so little is revealed about them, that Jesus *grew in wisdom and stature and in favour with God and men.'* This growth, physical, mental, social and spiritual happened in the confines of a small village, with a terrible reputation and with all the pressures and problems that running a small town business would bring. In this 'specially chosen' place Jesus grew and developed to become our Saviour and Great High Priest tempted in every way as we are and able to sympathise with us in our weaknesses. Little did the critics and those who despised Nazareth realise that in this maligned place the Saviour of the world grew to full manhood and would finally provide an affirmative answer to the question, *'can anything good come out of Nazareth?'*

Many 'life-lessons' were learned in Marshall and Anderson, lessons that would stand me in good stead for the work of the ministry. Every apprentice has to start at the bottom and for me the bottom, at the beginning of my training, was 'tea-boy', charged with the important responsibility of providing the men with tea at the correct temperature, at the correct colour and at the correct time and woe betide any boy who got any of them wrong. British engineering ran on tea!

The machine shop was a noisy and cold place, especially in winter, but it was also a tough place for a young Christian to take his stand for Christ and the determination to stay true to the Lord was often tested. I learned a lot about myself and about human nature. Alongside the machine shop was a cemetery and it proved to be a good quiet place at lunch time for an opportunity to read the Bible and pray.

I had no father to guide me in my formative years but the Lord provided some wonderful 'surrogate' fathers for me in those 'growing-up' years. I had wonderful examples and teachers in my first Pastor, Alex Tee, my Bible class teacher Joe Gray and other men like David Ayling, Jim McBurnie, Andy McHolm and Jim Wardrope. Those men and many others provided me with good male role models and with care and guidance when needed.

Saturday nights at Motherwell Elim were always 'deputation nights' and groups would come along to minister in song and testimony like The Ross Brothers from Kilsyth Westport Hall and I was motivated to learn the guitar. At 16 I had bought my first guitar and along with some other young men from the church we started taking meetings ourselves mainly in Glasgow City Missions and these provided me with my early preaching opportunities. It also provided the listeners with 'grace opportunities' as they endured my first attempts at preaching the Word.

At the age of 17 I met and fell in love with the young lady with whom I was to share the rest of my life. Margery Stewart not only caught my eye but also the eye of my mother who declared that 'she was the kind of young lady I would like to see you marry'. My mother was one of the biggest matchmakers in the Motherwell church but her instincts were only confirmed when Margery was one of her nurses during her final illness and she experienced first-hand her skills as a nurse.

I was attracted not only by Margery's beauty but also by her strong commitment to God and His Word, right from the day of her conversion. Margery was brought up in the village of Law. Her mother had the huge task of bringing up Margery and her two sisters and brother with no husband. He had been a miner but was killed in a rock fall six weeks before Margery was born. Both of us had upbringings that taught us the value of money and learning to 'get by' on meagre resources.

My mother died when I was 21 and shortly after that Margery and I got engaged. But such was Margery's commitment to God's will for her life that, even after five years of courtship, the night before the day we planned to get engaged she still wanted a final confirmation that it had God's approval, so we decided to pray once more and ask for a final word from the Lord. The next morning we met and asked if the Lord had spoken to us and He had. Both of us had been given a clear verse from the Bible and on comparing we found that we had both had the exact same verse! Finally Margery concluded that it was right for us to get engaged that day.

I had just opened my first bank account and had deposited £53 in it. The ring that Margery chose at H Samuel's cost £53; it cleaned out my newly opened account, but was worth every penny. It still graces her finger 53 years after I put it on her sitting on a bench in St George's Square in Glasgow. We were married on June 28, 1963, in the Motherwell Elim Church. Our wedding was a relatively low key event with the reception for 48 people in a local hotel costing the princely sum of £24 (50p per head). Alongside the astronomical sums spent on today's weddings this was a tiny amount, but it still stretched us financially as we were saving up for me to go to Bible College.

Bible College

We were only married for nine weeks when I left for the Elim Bible College in Clapham, London. Margery could not accompany me as she was in the middle of a midwifery course. So for most of the first year of our married life we were apart but this was wonderfully brought to a close by a broken leg I sustained from a motorbike accident which meant the last term of my first year in college was spent recuperating at home in Margery's village of Law.

I only made one trip to Scotland on my Ariel 250cc motorbike and the journey (pre-motorway days) took 15 hours and was extremely cold. At one point I encountered a terrible fog which resulted in me being reduced to driving down the middle of the road following the white line at a very slow speed. What I found disconcerting was the volume of traffic which was building up behind me impatiently flashing their lights and blowing their horns. I finally was forced over to the side of the road to allow them to speed off, very dangerously, into the thick fog. At the side of the road I took off my goggles and it was then that I discovered that the fog miraculously disappeared! There was no fog, my goggles were dirty! I have often used this story as an illustration of the importance of clear vision but I'm sure it has often left the listeners wondering about my state of mind and that's when I was young!

You make friendships in college which can last a lifetime and one such friend was Sid Sparks from South Africa. We entered into a pact that we would help each other maintain the habit of an early rise for devotions at the start of each day. We were like ghostly monks creeping around the college shrouded in blankets to try and keep warm as we went to our prayer times in a part of the college known as 'The Ark', specially set aside for prayer. It was a good habit that served me well throughout my ministry.

By my second year in college Margery had joined me in Clapham having completed the midwifery course she had been on. But then the College moved from Clapham to Capel in Surrey and for our last months in College we enjoyed the luxury of the new premises.

In the early 1960s going to Bible College as a married student was rare and certainly not encouraged. All students, on graduation, were expected to be single, free and able to go anywhere at short notice and 'unencumbered' by a wife. I think the requirement had its roots in the early days of Elim when the movement was expanding so rapidly that it needed the flexibility of single ministers emerging from training. College in 1963 was very different to Regents Theological College, our movement's current college, with no full time lecturers. Teaching was provided by Elim ministers coming for one week, starting their chosen subject on a Monday and finishing with an exam on a Friday. Wesley Gilpin, the College Principal, and his wife Marguerite worked tirelessly to improve on this and the dramatic difference in academic standards that we see today stand as a tribute to the foundation they laid back in the sixties.

College was a hugely enjoyable experience and being a guitar player I was soon involved in music ministry which saw us out most weekends. During my second year in college Margery worked in the Horsham Cottage Hospital which provided some very necessary income to help us to survive to the end of term. In those days students who applied to enter the Elim ministry had to preach in front of the Executive Council so for me and Denis Phillips, a fellow student and future minister, this took place at Croydon Elim Church at their mid-week Bible study. The Pastor, Willie Maybin, and the congregation did all they could to make it easy for us but the sight of a row of unsmiling and very serious Executive Council members filing into the back of the church did nothing to quieten the nerves. I (graciously) allowed Denis to go first!

The season for training very quickly came to an end and the exciting world of ministry was beckoning. My interview with the Executive Council seemed to have less to do with my calling to ministry and more to do with the fact I committed the sin of being a married student and also whether or not Margery could sing, play the piano or preach. After two years of study and the ordeal of the final interview with the Executive Council expectations were high as we had the Graduation service in Spurgeon's Tabernacle but as you will see in the next chapter things did not initially work out as expected.

My Chocolate Box Journey

2

Early Days in the Ministry

One of the defining features of 21st century life is the ever growing complexity of choice. It is part of the essence of modern living and with internet access people can very easily become aware of their huge variety of options. Even a simple thing like choosing toothpaste presents us with multiple choices and the need for extensive reading of labels to ensure we get the brand and type that best suits our personal requirements.

Oz Guinness in his book *The Call* challenges our obsession to choice with these words,

> '...*to be modern is to be addicted to choice. Choice for modern people is a right that overwhelms both responsibility and rationality and ultimately only one thing can conquer choice – being chosen. "I have chosen you," said Jesus, "you have not chosen me." We have no rights only responsibilities. Following Christ is not our initiative, merely our response in obedience. Once we have been called, we literally "have no choice".'*

39

When Jesus uttered the words to Peter, *'Follow me'*, his life changed for ever. His obedience to being chosen affected his business, his family life, his personal life and his future decisions. Today, because of the overload of multiple choices people can literally shape their religion and 'spirituality' to suit personal preference and lifestyle. But when the Jesus of the gospels confronts us, the awareness of His Lordship leaves no room for personal negotiation.

For Peter, *'follow me'* did not carry explanations or terms and conditions, expected benefits or career prospects. Rather it was a matter of *'take up your cross and follow me, deny yourself, lose yourself, forsake all'*, etc. This is hardly attractive headline grabbing stuff for 21st century choice and freedom addicts. The demands of discipleship have not lessened or been moderated to make them more attractive and acceptable to western hemisphere Christians. However, like a rich and successful young man who once came to Jesus to try and find a solution to his inner emptiness we still have the option to say 'no'.

Coming back to Peter and his call to follow Jesus; for him, at first, there would be a high level of excitement – a new venture, the crowds, miracles, travel, responsibility and the feeling of being 'in' at the start of a new movement for change. Within a short time, however, his attitude to commitment needed a course correction.

The unwillingness of the young man I have just mentioned to *'forsake all'* and follow Jesus suddenly awakened in Peter a conviction that his willingness to *'forsake all and follow'* (in the light of the other young man's unwillingness) must be worth significant rewards '...*we have left everything to follow you! What then will there be for us?*' (Matthew 19: 27). In reply, Jesus first answered the question and then with one of His amazing stories He answered the attitude behind the question. In the story that follows we get an insight into labour and work practices in pre-union days. But more importantly Christ reveals that in our following of Him the attitude of the heart is paramount, and even 'first called' people can end up being last if a bargaining spirit is allowed to creep in.

Before Margery said yes to my proposal of marriage in 1962 she had very carefully weighed up her willingness to become a part of my calling as well as a part of my life. Marrying a draughtsman was one thing but someone entering the full time ministry required a lot more thought. She had asked for, and received, clear confirmation from God that it was right for her to marry me and so was ready for the start of the 'ministry' journey when the college training years were over.

Before I go on to share with you some of my journey in ministry I need to warn against the distortion that sees people involved in what is regarded as 'the full-time ministry' as somehow more called and therefore more valued than people who are not. The sacred/secular divide is a man-made division.

We need to remind ourselves that every occupation is special to God. Jesus had the highest commendation from His Father at the end of His 'eighteen silent years' spent in obscurity when He preached no sermons and did no miracles. Yet His Father's assessment of His mundane life at work as a carpenter was, *'This is my Son, I love him and I am pleased with him.'*

Felixstowe

After graduation from Elim Bible College in 1965 instead of heading excitedly for our first ministry challenge we found ourselves back in Scotland. All the graduating students who wanted churches were placed, except us! So, it was back to nursing for Margery and for me, back to the drawing board in Marshall and Anderson. Finally, after months back in Scotland a phone call from Mr Morgan from Elim HQ at Clarence Avenue in Clapham informed me that I was requested to take on what he described as a 'church-with-a-challenge'. Felixstowe was the destination and the challenge was that it only had two people, a hired building, no salary and no accommodation.

The two people were Peter and Pat Adams 'on loan' from the Ipswich church to help us try and establish a church after an evangelistic crusade by Pastor Alfie Chewter, the minister at Ipswich Elim Church. Peter and Pat managed a retirement home in Felixstowe and offered us a room in the garret of the house with food and accommodation in return for help in the kitchen. It was winter and it was a very cold one with the only heating from a shilling in the slot 1KW heater – fortunately, however, the shilling dropped out every time so we were able to reuse it. But what did that matter? We were young, keen and determined to make a big difference in a very short space of time! Margery's experience in cooking was, to put it mildly, very limited, so when Pat took ill and Margery had to take over the kitchen it was a big test for everyone, not least the residents of the home. But we all survived.

As Christmas approached in our first church in Felixstowe things were looking quite bleak; money was tight so we were anticipating a Christmas dinner of mince and potatoes. Then, out of the blue, two members from the Ipswich Church, John and Cynthia, phoned to ask if we would like to spend Christmas with them. Would we? We jumped at the offer and what a feast they prepared; they lavished kindness (and calories) on us. The mince and potatoes would keep for another day.

We worked very hard in Felixstowe. Establishing a new church is not easy and Suffolk folk are reserved and proved very cautious of this enthusiastic guitar playing Scot. Peter and Pat were marvellous helps. Sometimes the congregation consisted only of Peter and Margery as Pat had to take their baby out. Despite the small number they got the full works – songs (accompanied by my guitar), prayers, readings, full length sermon and benediction! A lady called Norma joined us. She was American and her husband worked at the nearby US airbase. Norma was an amazing 'gatherer' and so before long we saw growth, mainly wives and children from the airbase.

The church grew and, like all small new church plants, it attracted the usual mix of interesting characters. We met the full spectrum at Felixstowe and with a growing awareness of our limitations our learning curve was very steep. When Norma arrived with her usual entourage of recent contacts we had no idea what kind of desperate human problems were going to come through the door and be presented to us for solving. It was a very 'interesting' time. Then there was Mr Booth, ex Salvation Army and he did look a bit like the original General Booth! He loved to play the piano (for 'play' you could substitute 'attack') and he also believed in greeting everyone with a thoroughly biblical and literal 'holy kiss'. No hand shake for him would suffice.

Norma's husband, Jack, didn't attend but he did lend me his very large American car on a Sunday. I used to pack twenty-one children into that car for the afternoon Sunday school and with nine in Peter's Morris Minor (no seat belt laws in those days!) we had a good healthy number of children present.

We finally moved from the garret to a small flat in the town and every Sunday afternoon most of the children stayed behind for tea at the 'Vicarage' so that they and some of their parents could come to church at night. The couple who owned the flat lived downstairs but instead of strongly objecting to this noisy invasion, every Sunday they would contribute food to feed the hungry mob and finally ended up coming to the church and became good friends for years afterwards. We certainly got our baptism of fire in Felixstowe but also had a great time and to this day Peter and Pat are two of our longest standing friends.

Money was incredibly tight. Anything left over after all church bills were paid would be my 'salary' so with an income of £9 and expenditure about the same we never had much to declare to the tax man. But we were happy, the church grew to about thirty and the job Margery eventually managed to get in an Ipswich hospital finally provided us with some income.

Then I became concerned when Margery began to be badly affected by the smell of cooking and even being in the kitchen. The truth was finally communicated to me that she was pregnant. On the one hand we were thrilled but on the other we wondered what was going to happen. The tiny flat we were in had a 'no babies' clause so accommodation and income were once again high on the agenda.

It was at this time that I received my second letter from James Morgan at Elim HQ. This time it was to inform me that I was being appointed as assistant minister to P S Brewster at Cardiff City Temple. In college P S Brewster's name was talked about in hushed tones of respect. He was at that time one of Elim's leading evangelists having pioneered many of the Movement's bigger churches and Cardiff, was then regarded as Elim's flagship church. The timing was 'providential'. Margery worked as long as she was able and, along with our few possessions, we arrived in Cardiff in time for the 1966 Easter Convention.

Cardiff

From Elim's smallest church to its biggest in one weekend! Cardiff City Temple Easter Conventions attracted people from all over the Principality and with the finest speakers and singers it was always a memorable event. It was also a marathon season of meetings starting with Thursday night, three on Good Friday, two on Saturday, four Sunday, three Monday, two on Tuesday and finishing on Wednesday. And with each meeting having two speakers we had scrambled brains by the end of it. I was shocked to discover that one of my duties as assistant was to train and conduct the 100 voice youth choir. Never having done anything like this before made me a quick learner.

Our ten years in Cardiff were wonderful, happy, exciting and offered me the unique opportunity to work very closely with an amazing evangelist and pastor. I soon became his chauffeur, gardener and general helper and shadow. I was able to accompany him on almost every conceivable kind of ministry. What a learning opportunity.

On one of the many journeys that I made with Mr Brewster he once came very close to laying hands on me in a less than biblical way. We had driven to Coventry for him to speak to the ministers of the British Pentecostal Fellowship.

One thing Mr Brewster could not stand was being late so I made sure I had him there in plenty of time. On the way up he had, as usual, discussed with me what he was going to say and as I had heard the sermon before I decided after dropping him I would park the car and take some time to go and have something to eat. He always bought me steak and chips after one of these journeys and so I decided to have my steak while the meeting was in progress. A suitable restaurant was found, the meal ordered, enjoyed, the daily paper read and I sauntered back to the hall only to discover a very angry P S Brewster pacing up and down on the corner where I had dropped him. 'You've taken me to the wrong hall,' he exploded. 'Where have you been?' When I lamely gave my explanations I thought I was going to be a GBH victim.

Next Sunday he had calmed down enough to tell the church of our trip to Coventry. The place was rocking with laughter and to try and restore some order to the place Mr Brewster called for the people to calm down and sing a song. The choice was unintentional and priceless. 'Man shall not live by bread alone' •

was his choice of chorus, which got an immediate response from the youth choir, 'nor by steak and chips'. The meeting closed unceremoniously and the story passed into folklore.

Mr Brewster was a hard worker and expected the same from his assistants. Thirty membership home visits had to be accomplished each week and people not at home did not count. The doors of the building had to be open one hour before each meeting and we were last to leave each night. Despite being such a large church Cardiff was a very happy church and relatively trouble free.

I learned so much from working closely with Mr Brewster and soon got to know when some personal correction was on the agenda. He would take me by the arm with the words, 'James, let's go for a walk', when another piece of wisdom was about to be added to my character. In later years I often thought of those occasions when I would preach on Peter's walk and talk with Jesus when the two of them had a 'heart-to-heart' after the resurrected Lord had cooked breakfast for him. 'Peter, let's go for a walk.' I could imagine it.

The Cardiff people were incredibly kind to us as a family but as well as generous and caring they also enjoyed church and loved fun. One year I forgot to change my clock and arrived very late at church for the morning service. Everyone, including Mr Brewster, had a lot of fun with me over it and for years afterwards, wherever we were in the country, we could depend on a large number of phone calls from Cardiff reminding us to 'change our clocks'.

I am married to an amazing woman, she is the wisest person I know, has great patience and has faced all the challenges of the ministry with cheerfulness and willingness. But even the most amazing of women have their limit and Margery once forced me to confront a serious shortcoming in my role as husband and father. It was a time when life for me was very busy and rewarding; I was out every evening as well as fully engaged in important Kingdom matters during the day. I was very happy and fulfilled but I forgot that at home was a young wife with three under school age children who was longing for some adult conversation and attention from a 'far-too-busy' husband who was helping to sort out lots of other people's problems but was failing to notice the problem that was growing in his own home – a wife who was suffering from quite bad post-natal depression.

Well, one night the frustration boiled over and I came home to a pile of broken china that had been smashed on the kitchen floor and it wasn't the working china, it was the best wedding china. The lesson was written in large letters – I had failed in my duty as a Christian husband. The fault was mine and I had to put it right. Fortunately, forgiveness is another of Margery's many attributes but as well as an apology there had to be a change of life-style and priorities. It took time but grace prevailed.

P S Brewster served in Cardiff for 35 years and his long-term commitment produced a remarkable and significant congregation of people who loved the Lord and His church. So many of the City Temple's outstanding people are worthy of mention but I will limit my experience to two.

Ken Barter was a train driver who, despite the fact he worked shifts always spent at least two hours per day waiting on God.

Ken always came to church with something from God for whoever the Lord brought to his mind in prayer. He ran a Sunday afternoon Bible Class for young men and to this day there are men in Cardiff, Wales and much further afield whose lives are still affected by his teaching.

Then there was Hector Jones a teacher of Welsh who had a very nervous disposition and a bad stammer. But when Hector was used in Prophecy he soared into heights of spiritual eloquence with no trace of a stammer. As his school was near where we lived he used to come round to visit us at lunch time. The spiritual wisdom imparted over those lunches was priceless. The memory and impact of men like Ken and Hector and a host of others like them had long term benefits in the lives of Margery and me.

Despite the fact that our ten years in Cardiff were incredibly happy ones in 1976 we knew it was time for us to leave and 'stand on our own two feet'. By this time Mr Brewster had left Cardiff and was serving as Elim's General Superintendent in Cheltenham. When I spoke to him about my desire to leave he said there was only one church available at that time and it was Kingstanding in Birmingham.

We had often driven through Birmingham on our annual pilgrimage to Scotland at New Year time and I had frequently commented to Margery that I hoped the Lord would never call us to Birmingham! Little did I realise the special blessing God had in store for us in Kingstanding.

Kingstanding

Bobby Morrison and his wife Joan had pastored the Kingstanding Elim Church for 25 years and by their love and exemplary care they had a very fine church. On hearing of their wonderful track record my nerves only increased further when I learned that they wanted to retire in the area and continue attending the church. On top of this I discovered that his son was Sunday School Superintendent, his son-in-law youth leader and a deacon and his daughter was the chief musician. Margery and I very quickly learned that our fears were groundless. Bobby and his wife, Joan, became the very best examples of how to support a new minister who did not do things the way they had always been done. Whenever I introduced a new programme Bobby Morrison was always first in line to 'sign up' for it.

I found out later that before I arrived Bobby had prayed over every seat in the building, anointed it with oil and asked God to fill every one of them with new converts. What an amazing couple they were and what a supportive family. They are still friends to this day.

When God began to fill the seats with new converts I knew whose prayers were being answered. God was answering the great prayers of a great man. It was an amazing season of growth and Pauline, one of our members, proved to be a marvellous witness among her neighbours. Whole families were getting saved and baptismal services were regular occurrences with father being first to be baptised and he would then help baptise his wife and children. They were days of great joy.

At my first baptismal service I was informed that it was customary for me to wear a long black robe with full length body wellingtons underneath. I reluctantly agreed but soon discovered that the boots leaked and when I came out of the water to finish the service and pronounce the benediction the water spouted out from the many holes. I was like a black water fountain. Everybody got a huge laugh and the robes and boots got a well-deserved and permanent retirement.

The Kingstanding people loved to sing and the meetings were incredibly joyful and full of life. Everyone was willing to work and participate and Sundays were days of expectancy as we all wondered what new miracle of grace God was going to do. Then one morning another of 'those' letters arrived from Cheltenham. This time from the Executive Council (now called the National Leadership Team) asking me to consider allowing my name to go forward to the annual Conference for the post of National Youth Director.

Eldin Corsie had been fulfilling this role as well as leading Kensington Temple and the Executive Council felt it was time for the position to be full time. My first reaction was that this was not the right time as things were going so well in Kingstanding, but after prayer and sharing it with the other leaders in the church we looked to God for His guidance.

The Sunday before the decision had to be made dawned and still no clear guidance. Margery and I as well as the leaders came to the morning meeting with a focussed need for help. Joan Morrison (Pastor Morrison's wife) had a remarkable gift of prophecy and interpretation and that morning, with no understanding of the decision that had to be made, she was prompted by the Holy Spirit to minister vocal gifts three times. By the conclusion of her ministry the leaders and Margery and I were left in no doubt that God was clearing the way for us to reluctantly leave Kingstanding and go to Cheltenham. So like the elders at Ephesus when Paul left we all said, *'the will of the Lord be done'*.

So in 1978 after only a two year stay in Kingstanding we said our very tearful farewells to the many new converts and friends we had made and with a lot of trepidation headed south to a completely different kind of challenge as Elim's National Youth Director.

3

Widening Horizons

One of my favourite New Testament characters is Philip, the only man to be designated as an evangelist. This man's journey from new convert in Jerusalem to international evangelist makes for great reading. His roots in the exciting and fast growing church in Jerusalem laid the foundation for his rapid rise to an effective and far reaching public ministry. Philip started out on his spiritual journey among that great crowd of new converts in Jerusalem as they gave close attention to the foundation of the Apostle's doctrine, prayer, fellowship and breaking of bread. These are still essential foundations for any 21st century convert. It is obvious that Philip stood out among the converts in Jerusalem for when seven exceptional men were required to become assistants to the Apostles and care for widows Philip was an immediate and obvious choice. He fulfilled all the qualifications for this first New Testament 'deaconing' role which were – 'from among them' (a member of the church), full of the Holy Ghost and wisdom and a man of unblemished public character as well.

Then the unthinkable happened; the church in Jerusalem was scattered when persecution hit them as a result of Stephen's testimony and Philip was forced to leave his home church. It was then the latent gift of the evangelist became obvious in his choice of place he headed to – Samaria; a place on God's agenda but up until that moment not on the church's agenda. It was obvious that Samaria's time for a Holy Ghost visitation had come and, as a result of Philip preaching Christ, the city was revolutionised by the joy that comes from gospel freedom. From Philip's willingness to submit to Apostolic instruction and to serve the needs of others came the explosive fruitfulness of a life open to God's 'surprises' and his unexpected choice of a place for revival.

National Youth Director

As I moved from the role of local Pastor to the wider itinerant role as National Youth Director, the life of Philip was challenging me to lift my horizons. As I looked at the developing life of this sometimes overlooked New Testament character I began to be aware of the lesson of Jerusalem. This wonderful first New Testament church which experienced amazing grace and growth had a serious flaw – it failed to follow through on the (Great) Commission that Christ had given them – Jerusalem, Judea, Samaria and the uttermost parts of the earth. Despite the incredible blessing that Jerusalem experienced and the courage and boldness the believers exhibited, they were still confined to Jerusalem several years after Pentecost. Judea, far less Samaria or the uttermost parts of the earth, had not yet appeared on their mission's agenda. God had to resort to a very drastic method to shake them out of the Jerusalem salt cellar.

The catalyst for change was an amazing sermon by Stephen, one of Philip's fellow 'servers'. Stephen was a rising star in the Jerusalem church, possibly a future CEO. His sermon was a bold recounting of national rebellion culminating in their crucifixion of Christ the Messiah. It was the tipping point and more than the pious religious leaders could stomach, it stirred up incredible hatred. The reaction revealed the religious leaders in their true colours – *'When they heard this they were furious and gnashed their teeth at him...yelling at the top of their voices they rushed at him and dragged him out of the city and began to stone him (to death).'*

The result was that the geographically restricted Church became unrestricted, it was a painful experience but the end result was good – *'they were scattered throughout Judea and Samaria....those who were scattered preached the word wherever they went'.* They went to the places they were supposed to go to and did what they had been commanded to do. The enjoyable church life-style of Jerusalem was severely disturbed but the commission of Christ was being fulfilled.

As I got into my role as Youth Director I was beginning to ask serious questions about the church in the UK. It was going to take drastic action to shake the church out of the smug comfort zone style that was so dependent on plenty of blessing, protection, risk-free and cost-free Christianity so that rather than declining in size and influence the church in the UK could once again become the force for change in the nation. Gavin Reid, the author and former Anglican bishop made a telling comment when he described the modern church as the greatest 20th century idolatry.

For me, my time as Elim's National Youth Director was certainly a season of expanding horizons, new and bigger challenges, travel and the opportunity to be exposed to the wider work of the Kingdom of God. Up until this time my ministry had been confined to the local church but now I had the chance to see what was happing nationally and internationally It was a hugely enjoyable time with national initiatives like *The Year of the Family*, *The Year of the Sunday School*, leading the Youth Choirs in the Royal Albert Hall, National Youth rallies and Elim Youth camps. During this time the Youth Department launched a new youth magazine called *Bread*. For its day it was very cutting edge and dared to deal with difficult and sometimes controversial subjects. It was sometimes hard to balance submission to those in leadership above me with the enthusiasm of the two young editors – Peter Sanderson and Alistair Forrest who were so keen to bring Biblical light to difficult issues.

It was during this time that Brian Edwards, Director of Elim Missions and the Youth Department combined to launch the Euro Teams – teams of young people heading for churches in Europe to assist them in their evangelistic outreach. On one of the first trips to Udine in Italy the mini bus had a problem with its suspension and the passengers all had to sit on one side of the bus. It so happened that one young Scottish lady ended up sitting on the knee of a young man from Northern Ireland, love blossomed on the difficult journey, they got married (not on the trip) and lived very happily ever after. Don't you just love a good ending? On these organised trips to Europe many young people got a taste for missions work and some eventually headed off to the mission field. The teams usually stayed in our home before they set off and when they got back so it was always a joy to feel the anticipation as they started off and the buzz of excitement when they returned. There is nothing like involvement in missions to help keep your heart on fire for the Lord. Try it, you won't be disappointed.

Bristol Days

After three exciting years as National Youth Director, in 1981 another chocolate was about to be unwrapped and this one would take me into one of the most stretching and challenging seasons of my life thus far.

The seventies and eighties saw the emergence of what came to be known as 'the house church movement' and Elim began to feel the effect on some of our churches chaffing at what they regarded as restrictions and bad biblical practice. Issues like the biblical role of elders, law and grace and what was permissible for Christians to do or not do, dancing, drinking wine, freedom etc became 'hot topics'. Some of the people who eventually broke away from Elim were good friends of mine and I had long discussions with them on why these issues need not be divisive. With the benefit of hindsight now it is easy to see that more toleration on Elim's side along with willingness to explore the issues as well as some patience on their side could have resulted in a lot less painful separations. Change is always painful. For me it was a time to examine long held beliefs and practices and sort out what was my cultural background and what was a principal of Scripture. It wasn't always an easy distinction to make.

At this time I became gripped by a strong desire to begin to see church as He wanted it and not an expression of what suited me. Antioch became my favourite New Testament church – how it started, its evangelism, its social concern, its leadership composition, its pastoral care, its teaching programme, and of course its ground breaking missions outreach that started the gospel message on its journey to the 'ends of the earth'. I became convinced (and still am) that church has the potential to be the greatest force for good change in society. Despite being a great church Jerusalem failed to follow through on the last recorded words spoken by Jesus *'go and make disciples of all nations'*. The sermon of Stephen in front of the religious leaders was the flash point for an outbreak of persecution; it was also the point of a breakthrough in world evangelisation.

Out of the fire came fruitfulness. An Australian guide once told me that one of their trees will not be fruitful until it passes through the fire. It seems that the fire causes the seed pods to open and 'spit out' the seeds for a distance of two to three metres from the parent tree so that they will not encroach on the mother tree's nutrients while the smoke from the fire causes the seed to germinate. Some of the seeds of the fire in Jerusalem were spat-out as far as Antioch and so commenced that amazing prototype which created a different church style in so many areas. Antioch provided the 'wine-skin' for the new wine that God was pouring out. Little did I know that I was about to participate in a modern 'Antioch-style' church.

The change in direction for Margery and I came in the form of another of those 'letters' from HQ. I was invited to consider allowing my name to go forward to be considered for leadership of the Bristol City Temple and take over from

Archie Biddle, one of Elim's most respected senior ministers who was retiring. After prayer and an interview with the fifteen elders I accepted the invitation.

At first my time in Bristol seemed to go well and numbers steadily increased to nearly 400, but I became aware of serious shortcomings in what was expected of me as the leader. Far too much was expected from the 'paid professional' and in most meetings it was all platform led. I was at last coming to the blatantly obvious truth that the task of a church leader is not to do all the work but to equip the saints for the work of the ministry – coaching and training people to be worshippers, workers and witnesses. I realised that I barely knew the names of the people in the congregation far less their spiritual condition. This style of 'doing' church had to change.

As a start I prepared a discussion document for the fifteen elders on the need for small groups but also the essential preparation of training up small group 'pastors' to assist in the care of the people. The proposal was thoroughly discussed and after a time of reflection the answer came back from the majority of the fifteen elders that this could never be the way ahead. Maybe I should have been more patient in introducing this 'radical' change but the level of intransigence was strong and solid.

After reflection and considering the level of opposition to any change my reaction was to resign and allow them to find a leader who would go in the direction they desired. I realised that what was in my heart would be contentious. However five of the leaders indicated that they wanted to press on with change. After a long and difficult discussion with all the leaders concerned and with the Executive Council it was agreed that since Bristol was such a big city it could stand two Elim Churches. It was therefore agreed that a new fellowship would be formed and would commence on the 23rd of January 1982 with each church being free to express its own style of church. The people of the City Temple were free to make a choice and on our first Sunday morning 90 people gathered in Begbrook Primary school.

During those early months in Begbrook I came into contact with some remarkable leaders in the city of Bristol, men like Robert Scott-Cook and Graham Loader who became very supportive friends. Both of these men had their roots in the Brethren movement but after coming into an experience of the Holy Spirit they exhibited that wonderful combination of being men of the Word and the Spirit. Other men like Andrew Truter of Fishponds Baptist Church, Malcolm Widdecombe (later Canon Widdecombe) of 'Pip-n-Jay' (St Philip and St Jacob Church) were incredibly supportive in the early days of the new church. What a delightful and unique Church of England vicar Malcolm was. He took on Pip-n-Jay when it was about to close and now it is one of the foremost churches in Bristol with a breath taking annual mission's budget. Malcom has now gone to his well-deserved reward in heaven.

The lessons and experiences of Bristol require a separate book but I hope the next chapter will, at least, give a flavour of those special days.

Wedding: Jim and Margery on their wedding day,
June 28, 1963 in the Motherwell Elim Church

Rev Duncan Campbell
of the Hebridean Revival
who prayed with Jim when
he became a Christian

A visit from Dr David Yonggi Cho of South Korea, with the ministerial team at
Cardiff City Temple: P.S.Brewster, Ramon Hunston and Jim Dick

Jim and Margery with their children Yvonne, Andrew and Lorraine

The girls: Yvonne and Lorraine

Lorraine during her time in Bangladesh

Lorraine with some of the medical team she worked alongside while with
VSO in Bangladesh

Margery, Yvonne and Joseph, Yvonne's son

Jim on a ministry trip to the Philippines

4

An Exciting New Church

The new church was due to commence in January of 1982 and as a part of my personal preparation I had gone to a Leader's Week at a centre called 'The Hyde' in Sussex. The week was led by church leaders and speakers Bob Gordon and Colin Urquhart and proved to be one of those 'turning point' experiences in my life.

At the first meeting of the week all the leaders got their note-books out preparing to 'capture' any good thoughts for future sermons. Bob Gordon stood up and told us, no *commanded* us, 'Put your note-books away as you here to meet with God not just get ideas for Sunday's sermon!' So the note-books were hurriedly put away!

The teaching on motivation in leadership was very searching. One morning there were about 120 of us worshipping in a room and a young man began to play on the keyboard as we waited on God. As he played it became obvious that what was coming out was not from his own skill. It was as if a window had been opened in heaven and we were listening to heaven's music. It lasted for several minutes and when finally the music stopped 120 leaders were on their faces in the manifest presence of God. Truly awesome!

The new church which began meeting in Begbrook Primary School and was called New Life Fellowship quickly began to grow and had a wonderful mix of members. There were two main groups that challenged our thinking and stretched our ability to adapt. We had a great group of Jamaicans as well as established Bristolians. The worship of Jamaicans is far less inhibited than that of traditional Anglo Saxons. It soon became obvious that allowing cultural expressions of worship was going to present us with challenges. We concluded, however, that if we were going to be a New Testament style church after the Antioch sort we would need to allow for and welcome a variety of worship styles. We began to enjoy the best distinctives from both and a lot of grace and patience meant the fellowship became the stronger for our diversity.

Another group which contributed to our growing unity in diversity was the lads from *Life for the World* – a drug rehabilitation centre that had made New Life their home church. It was the era of Mohican haircuts and other 'distinctive' expressions of style. It was strange and amusing on a Sunday to see some very large and visually intimidating ex-addicts sitting next to some of our very sedate and well-dressed senior ladies. Needless to say some felt very intimidated by the presence of the lads from *Life for the World* and the problem was especially acute when communion was being served from a communal cup. The lads believed in taking a very satisfying amount of the non-alcoholic wine but when the cup was passed to the sedate ladies all the stories of Aids transmission, which was very much in the news at the time and not well understood, came into focus. We got some very anxious comments and suggestions about a separate meeting for the lads but once again with a lot of patience and grace integration took place making the church the stronger for it. It became one of my pleasures on a Sunday to see these recently converted young men sitting together with some of our older ladies who had lived very sheltered lives but were becoming like the grandmothers that some of the lads never had.

The early days of the new church were exciting but with more than enough challenges to keep us praying and learning. It was a time of growth, not just numerically, but more importantly in our understanding of what church really was about.

Another significant contributing factor in the development of the church was the annual church holiday to Cornwall. We learned that the church that could laugh together could better worship together. It would not be an exaggeration to say that these holidays were a major contributing factor to the wonderful climate in the church meetings. They were, of course, expertly planned and executed by Peter Standerwick, our amazing and highly organised church administrator. What a gift Peter was to the church, a policeman by day but at all other times a committed and very hard working planner and organiser. He was every leader's dream of an administrator, meticulous and thorough, yes, but also very funny with it as well.

At this time we were learning the benefit of doing church without a church building. It's amazing how much architecture can affect atmosphere. The contrast between worshipping in a department store and a loaned and very ancient Church of England building was hard to believe. We learned to be at home in all kinds of buildings – schools, a theatre, a museum, borrowed halls and even a swimming pool. Joining the New Life Fellowship always guaranteed a free tour of some of Bristol's lesser known places. Not having our own building, however, did present us with problems especially when it came to funerals, weddings and other special functions, but we benefitted from the generosity of previously mentioned churches like Pip-n-Jay, Fishponds Baptist and others.

Everything we did had freshness about it – leadership meetings that you looked forward to, Sunday meetings that were not predictable, the presence of God that was 'tangible', sacrificial giving on a new scale. People came to church on a Sunday with the thought, 'I wonder what God is going to do today?' It was not uncommon for visitors to walk in on a Sunday and be profoundly moved emotionally, ask for help to get to know God and be prayed for, and all before the meeting got under way or I had even preached (humbling!). So much work was done by the Holy Spirit before the meetings began and so many financial needs were privately and anonymously met. It would be true to say that thousands of pounds moved around from givers to needy people. The testimonies of met needs were always wonderful.

But it was more than just financial needs that were being met. One couple who we thought were married turned out not to be married but on 'discovery' confessed their deception before the whole church and the lady, because of previous church experiences, fully expected to be humiliatingly expelled from the church. What a response followed though – the whole congregation all went forward to embrace them, express forgiveness and make them know they were still loved. It was not long until another one of the many church weddings took place.

Many of the couples getting married could not afford expensive weddings but that's when the whole church got involved and a complete and very inexpensive wedding service became available even down to lovely cars with chauffeurs with grey suit and cap!

The leadership were a dream team and what a mix of race, age and gifting. The 'daddy' of us all was Paul Clark and if ever there was a modern day Barnabas, he fitted the description. He 'oozed' (old Greek word!) love for people. Paul's favourite greeting was 'hello sunshine' and I later discovered that he really did this because he could never remember names so 'sunshine' was a safe name for everyone!

The unity, commitment and quality of the leadership were a major factor in the developing quality of the church. Hedley was the 'senior' in the team, from a very traditional background but a wonderful stabilising influence and possessing a dry but keen sense of humour. Lynton and Junior were two young Jamaican men who quickly rose in spiritual stature and had total commitment to God and the fellowship, and then there was Reg, Richard and David – men who were faithful and dependable. You've been introduced to Peter and Paul, later I will introduce you to Larry and Robert.

Our leadership meetings lasted for three hours and included our wives. The first hour was sharing from the Word, the second hour the ladies would pray while the men went off to another room to do some 'business' and the last hour was food, fun and fellowship! We were strict on time-keeping as most had jobs to go to the next day.

I was seeing the emergence of a modern-day Antioch in front of my eyes. All the characteristics of Antioch – its evangelism, its mix of people, its leadership, its social concern, its worship, the prophetic, ministry to other churches and its mission involvement – it was all there and very exciting. One of the leaders and his wife, Robert and Shirley Barfoot, began to feel the call of God to leave a very well paid and comfortable life-style, sell their home in the best part of Bristol and go and live in the most deprived part of Bristol to engage in inner city evangelism. It was a very hard and courageous thing to do, to leave a beautiful home in a prime area and go to live in the red-light district of St Paul's. What amazing courage and obedience but little did they realise that this was all part of the preparation for the call to a much bigger and wider work in Poland where they ministered for many years. Another leader, Larry O'Mahoney, one of the most natural evangelists I know, was instrumental in bringing many people into the church. Later he and his wife went to Southern Ireland where they serve as evangelists with Open Air Campaigners.

While the blessing and presence of God was incredibly refreshing this was counterbalanced by a lot of pressure caused by the problems associated with starting a new church in the same city with the parent church not many miles away. We also discovered that a new church always attracts a collection of people with some odd views and practices who are looking for a 'platform' to minister on. This kept the leadership team on their toes guarding the fellowship against the disruption that such people can often cause.

New Life was more than just the establishing of another new church to add to Bristol's many churches; we learned many lessons in those early pioneer days. So what was it that was different?

We learned that good church was not dependent on a purpose built building. As I previously said we met in all sorts of places – schools, theatre, museum, redundant Church of England building, a floor of the co-operative department store, swimming baths, homes etc. Church is all about people not property.

Another lesson was that quality of relationships was paramount especially among the leaders and unity of vision and purpose for the whole fellowship focussed our time, energy and resources.

Church was an enjoyable experience. Sunday was a day to be looked forward to, there was a lot of laughter and fun and spontaneous reactions like when it was a nice day outside at Begbrook we would go out onto the grass and have church 'al fresco'. It was a time of great freshness, new challenges, joyful sharing and authentic worship that attracted the presence and power of God.

Variety was something to be celebrated and embraced. There was no such thing as a 'normal' or 'standard' member – all kinds of people found acceptance in the fellowship. People participation was encouraged and spontaneous testimonies were a regular part of Sunday worship. The style of Sunday worship was less structured; meetings were unpredictable and very spontaneous. We never really knew what was going to happen in any meeting.

There was a strong emphasis on mission – Robert and Shirley Barfoot and their call to work in St Paul's, Larry O'Mahoney with Open Air Campaigners on the streets of Bristol, ten per cent of our income was given to Elim overseas missions (on top of the usual ten per cent to HQ) and the church supported me on mission trips to Africa.

In our early days John and Marilyn Glass joined us (now who's name dropping?) and became part of the leadership. John's gifting in evangelism was a significant contribution to the church's growth and his unique and outstanding style of preaching enhanced and enriched us as well. On one occasion John and I had been away for three days to seek God on a particular issue and when we came back we couldn't make up our minds as to who should minister on the Sunday so we decided to both preach and had our first chance at 'tag' preaching. It was an incredible experience and the church loved it!

While not having a building taught us a lot of spiritual lessons about church it also presented us with a lot of logistical problems so we decided to start preparing for a future purchase if that was to be God's will. We approached the fellowship to ask them to prepare for a 'one-off' special offering to start the building fund. After a few weeks of teaching and time for preparation the Sunday dawned for the special offering. People had gone to amazing lengths to raise money. One man sold his recently acquired and long awaited sports car, bought a much cheaper car and released money for the offering. One lady brought, for us to sell, the biggest diamond I have ever seen, her late husband had bought it for her as an investment for the future. We took it to a London auction house to have it valued and finally sold it in Bristol for a lot of money. Margery and the ladies had some fun trying it on and I thought I would need to have it surgically removed from their fingers to get it sold. I was humbled by the sacrificial generosity of every member and when the day dawned for the special offering the magnificent sum of £55,000 was raised which, considering the make-up of the congregation and the fact it was 25 years ago, was a magnificent one.

The Bristol New Life days were probably the most challenging, stretching and satisfying of my ministry. They certainly gave me a glimpse of a new kind of church culture that came very close to what I discovered in my study of The Acts of the Apostles and particularly the church at Antioch. It was one of those unique seasons in life that left an indelible imprint on the lives of all who were involved. I think it would be true to say that none of us who were in leadership have ever been the same since our pioneer days in Bristol New Life Church.

My Chocolate Box Journey

5

Regents Theological College

In 1988 I was approached by Elim's General Superintendent, Wynne Lewis, to ask if I would take on the task of Principal of Elim's Training College which at that time was at Nantwich (now in Malvern). My initial response was to say no, but after more prayer and a further approach from Wynne, I agreed. This appointment had to receive the approval of the Elim Conference so in the summer of 1988 and after Conference approval, Margery and I moved to Nantwich.

In many ways it was a very difficult move – leaving a church that meant so much to us but also leaving our family behind as well. They were all of age to now make their own decisions so the family stayed on in Bristol and Mum and Dad moved out!

Our children, Yvonne, Lorraine and Andrew had gone through a number of moves over the years which always involved new schools, new friends and new churches but they now felt it was time to put some roots down in Bristol. Yvonne worked in an office, Lorraine was a nurse and Andrew had started a career in insurance plus they had many friends in the Bristol Church and the thought of living in a college did not appeal to them. The move to the college also turned out to be a very difficult one for Margery, leaving the church and the leaders' wives to whom she was very close and the family – it was an emotional time for her.

Going to the college was more than a geographical move – it was a major life-style change for us. Moving into communal life for a pair of forty something-year-olds and having responsibility for an extended family of 200+ was different to normal church life.

When we arrived we initially had no home to go to so we moved temporarily into a guest room in the main building. One night we had just settled down to sleep when we heard a loud Scottish voice outside in the corridor and the next thing we knew the door of our bedroom opened and one of the students came in to show some friends the college guest room and the new Principal and his wife became part of the tour. To protect his anonymity we'll call him Paul S. You can imagine the shock he got (never mind the shock we got) when my voice boomed out from the darkness – 'Paul, what are you doing?' I caught up with him half-way down the corridor and an early morning meeting in my office was arranged.

The next morning word had got around and the whole college had found something to be doing in the corridor that morning, while Paul awaited my arrival. I managed to keep my laugh in and a stern face until we got into my office. Paul, of course, protested that he did not know we were sleeping in the room but it didn't stop him starting the story that I had Mickey Mouse pyjamas and Margery had her head covered in rollers and her teeth in a glass beside the bed (neither of which are true, Margery hastens to add). The story has passed into college folklore and no doubt has been embellished in the telling.

I quickly learned to love college life but at first I thought I had landed in a hot-bed of heretics when I had lunch with the faculty. It took me time to learn that they loved to provoke discussion with each other by making the most outrageous statements, not because they believed them but just to enliven the lunch table discussions. Once I grasped this I was able to relax and enjoy the marvellous debates they had as 'iron sharpened iron'. The faculty at that time were a marvellous group of people, totally dedicated to the teaching of the Word and academic excellence. We made a good team – I could not come anywhere near them in academics but I had a lot of experience in practical church life so together we had something really worthwhile to give to the enquiring minds of the students.

This was the beginning of a ministry very different to anything we had done before. I have been a life-long student of the Word but I am not an academic and I would now be working alongside colleagues who had more letters after their names than I had in the whole of my name.

My PA was Jackie Griffiths, who is now a missionary in Malawi, and one day she came into my office with a very big grin on her face. 'I have just been in the archives,' was her explanation. I replied with something about that being sad and that she needed to get out more often. 'I found your file from when you were a student at the first London College,' she said and then informed me with a smile, 'you didn't do very well as a student did you?' I made a lame explanation that my low average was due to missing a whole term's exams due to a motor bike accident. It didn't impress her very much but she did promise never to let the students know. Imagine what they would have done with that piece of information.

It was during my time at the college that the faculty was enhanced by the addition of Dr Siegfried Schatzmann, a very highly qualified ex-student of the original Elim Bible College in London. The college had decided to go for validation, initially with the Open University, and Siegfried had the know-how and ability to steer us through the complicated process of raising the college to the required standard. It was a tough and very demanding process for all concerned but the validation was achieved which now allows the present day college to teach to PhD level.

I was assigned to teach the course on Pastoral Theology, a subject I relished and I had a great time exploring, with the students, the many aspects of church ministry. I knew what they would be facing when they left the protected cloisters of Regents and wanted to give them the best start possible. We had fun teaching them how to perform weddings, dedications and funerals with real couples, babies but thankfully no bodies. Margery spent time with the wives giving practical advice on the role of a leader's wife.

College wasn't all study and hard work; it had good fun times as well. These were especially important after exam times when tensions and pressures were high so organised fun-days were marvellous tension diffusers – lots of water and mess to clear up after some wonderful water fights. The college had its share of practical jokers who gave us a healthy dose of pranks. One day my car developed a strange and loud whistling sound when the engine was running. I could not find the source of this irritating sound, nor could the garage, but at last the problem was solved – an unnamed student had fitted a metal ring inside my exhaust pipe which caused the whistling sound. I never did find out who did it but if you are reading this now it is not too late to confess, you will feel a lot better if you 'get it off your chest'.

Football was a popular sport for many of the students but there were times when their enthusiasm and passion overflowed into aggression. Margery became well known at Crewe's accident and emergency department with a steady stream of broken bones and other results of over-aggressive tackling. There was an occasion when I had to ban it for a time to let tempers cool down. It was interesting to observe students who could be so positive in worship changing into a totally different person when they put on a football strip and got a ball at their feet.

We had a dog while in college and every morning I used to walk Prince while the early morning work period was in progress – students were required to do thirty minutes of practical work before breakfast every morning. The students would see me walking around the grounds with Prince and thought that this was all there was to it, but I had picked up a pearl of wisdom from Mr Gilpin who was my Principal when I was a student. He used to do the same but he found it gave him a chance to watch the students at work, his theory was that a student's attitude and diligence to menial tasks was an indicator of what their attitude would be to bigger Kingdom tasks. I adopted the same idea and found the morning walks were very illuminating.

The highlight of the year was always the well-attended Graduation Service; it was quite a feat fitting 1000 people into the sport's hall. One year I was introducing one of the students to give a testimony of his call to Nepal, I gave him a glowing introduction and then I had what can only be described as a pre-senior moment – I could not remember his name. Needless to say the students thought it was priceless and the student concerned reminds me of it to this day. You get quite close to students when you are with them consistently and closely for up to three years, so the 'Commissioning' at the Graduation Service could be very moving as hands were laid on them, sending them out to fulfil the call of God on their lives.

College life had a very predictable routine to it, so come the summer break when students had left it was always a time I looked forward to for study, course preparation and reading, the things I had limited time for during the busy term time.

Regents had a marvellous mix of students from the UK, Europe and the world and this served to provide a marvellous training ground for Christian unity. When new students arrived the faculty would meet with them to help prepare them for the course ahead. I would speak about the challenge of getting on with each other as well as the challenge of study. I used to recite a little poem I had picked up somewhere:

> To dwell above with saints we love
> That will indeed be glory;
> But to dwell below with saints we know
> Well, that's another story.

Learning tolerance and patience with others who had different theological view points as well as standards and culture was a big challenge, especially to those who had only known a very defined set of rules and theological interpretation. It made for some very interesting discussions and debates but it contributed to the overall learning experience.

One student, a lady of 76 and an ex-school teacher, loved doing assignments and essays, she was always asking the lecturers for more home-work. A few of the students had to take her aside quietly and ask her to ease back on the public requests for more work as they didn't share her same passion for essays and assignments. Another student had been the Commander of a nuclear submarine and served in the Falklands conflict. It was quite a challenge for him to go back into a classroom with an above average number of young students but he completed the course and went out to fulfil God's will for his life.

And then there was a young lady from Switzerland who arrived at the college for an interview. She had been born with severe physical disabilities; her arms were undeveloped as also one of her legs. It was obvious she would need a lot of support to function in college life. After a lot of discussion and prayer we accepted her as a student and she went on to be an incredible inspiration to all the students. Very little stopped her; it was amazing to see her sitting on a desk (not at it) with a pen in one foot, writing her notes and a marker in the other foot underling pages. She had a very supportive group of students who compensated for the things she could not do. One of the carpenters made her a specially adapted stool so she could get up on to it and use her nose to press the buttons to get entry to the student block. She completed the course and gained her degree and the resounding cheers from the 1000 strong audience when she went on to the platform to receive her degree was deafening. She accepted it with her mouth! What an amazing example of courage and overcoming faith. She went back to Switzerland, gained another degree and continues to serve God today. When she came for her interview it would have been easier to say that she could not undertake the course due to the practical challenges but how much inspiration and example we would have denied the college if we had made that decision.

With up to 200 people living in community, a Theological College, a Day Nursery, an English Language School and a Conference Centre, an army of support staff was required to keep the place running smoothly. I saw as one of my responsibilities the task of endeavouring to keep all the departments moving in a similar direction so that the college could achieve its primary goal of training men and women for ministry. Not always an easy task especially when it came to allocating budgets and the college budgets at that time were in the very experienced hands of Malcolm Hathaway. He seemed to have the ability to stretch meagre resources to meet the many demands made on them.

Another area of pressure was the kitchen and the chef and his team had the unenviable task of trying to satisfy the huge variety of tastes demanded by students from so many different countries. The day that black pudding was on the menu sparked off some very intense theological debates. As far as I am aware it only appeared that once on the menu.

College was interesting, stretching, exciting and enjoyable but after six years I was missing involvement in regular church life in the world outside the college walls. One of the dangers I encountered was a feeling of living in the unreal world of college life. I enjoyed the experience of preparing men and women for ministry but I was missing that ministry myself.

It was at this time that an opportunity arose for Margery and I to go back to Scotland to serve as Regional Superintendent for the Scottish Elim Churches. I would be following John Glass who was relinquishing the post of Scottish RS to assume the leadership of the Kilsyth Church of God, the first full time leader the church had in its long and distinguished history. So in 1993 Margery and I found ourselves in Scotland, thirty years after leaving to go to Bible College as a student.

Another very interesting chocolate from our box was about to get unwrapped.

6

Back to Scotland

It had been a big culture shock leaving Scotland in 1963 but returning, thirty years later, was a reverse culture shock. A lot had change since that first journey south to Bible College. On returning, it was good to reconnect with many long-term friends from our growing up days in Scotland and two of our oldest friends were Myra and Ian Anderson and on a quick one-day visit Ian took a day off work to help us find accommodation. Well, by the end of the day amazingly, we had found a beautiful newly built bungalow to rent and sorted a car as the one I was driving belonged to the college. It was a good start to a new season in the land of my birth.

When John Glass relinquished his role as Regional Superintendent for Scotland he handed over all the Regional files and the Regional computer and learning to use a computer was a new challenge, for me. John was very computer literate and I was not so his five minute hand-over lesson did not make much of a dent on my computer illiteracy.

The Scottish Elim Churches were spread from Alness, which is north of Inverness, to Castle Douglas on the borders so a lot of time was spent in my new car, however, the sheer pleasure of being in the Highlands more than made up for the many hours spent driving, I sometimes had to pinch myself to remind me that it was real and not a dream. Life as a Regional Superintendent was varied, I had a responsibility to care for the pastors and leaders who cared for others, so time spent sitting with a pastor and his wife was important, it was a chance to allow them to talk about the stresses and joys of their church. It was also a chance to discuss strategies for growth and expansion and to find ways to help sharpen their leadership skills.

Sunday and mid-week visits to the churches plus regular Regional events and these, added to the home visits, allowed me to get to know the pastors and leaders and constantly underlined to me the quality and dedication of the men and women who serve our churches. It became a great privilege to be allowed to walk closely with them in the good times and when they faced difficult situations. God never fails to record every act of selfless service done for Him and the day will come when what was done in private will be rewarded openly.

As I previously mentioned, my father died when I was twelve and my brother had gone off to the war when I was born; he returned safely but then he headed for Africa to follow a career in map making. So in my formative years I lacked a male influence in my life but God very kindly made up for this by introducing into my life good male role models from my local church, men who watched out for me and were good examples for me to follow. It made me realise the importance and the powerful influence that solid, mature Christian men can be in the church, especially to young men. Sadly, many churches do not have an abundance of such men so I began to feel the need to do something to help strengthen the role of men in our churches. It was from this desire that *Covenant Men Network* was birthed.

My desire was to provide the men of the Scottish Elim Churches with good teaching material that would provoke them to the highest and best living for the Lord in their homes, in the church and in the work place. A conspiracy of issues have devalued and weakened the role of men – absent fathers, militant feminism, dehumanising job pressures, TV's portrayal of men and social trends and changes. In my desire to help men I was convinced of the central role the Word of God must play in the teaching of men and one verse in particular was key to what I wanted to achieve – 2 Timothy 3:15, *'All Scripture is God-breathed and is profitable for teaching, rebuking, correcting and training in righteousness so that the man of God may be thoroughly equipped for every good work.'*

I was also struck by a verse in Jeremiah that emphasised God's search for men who will make a difference – Jeremiah 5:1, *'If I can find one man who deals honestly and seeks the truth I will save this city.'* Ezekiel 22:30 also underlines this same search by God – *'I sought for a man...who would stand before me in the gap in behalf of the land so that I would not have to destroy it.'*

God can use a small number of committed, obedient men to make a profound impact on our cities and nations, remember Gideon with only three hundred men defeated a vastly superior army and saved Israel from annihilation. I spent quite a long time writing a teaching programme based on the Beatitudes which I consider to be a precise concentration of the teaching of Jesus. The title, *Covenant Men,* was inspired by the Scottish Covenanters from the seventeenth century, a group of men (and women) who bound themselves together by a covenant, often signed in their own blood, to oppose the imposition of a system of church order that sought to elevate a king to be the head of the church when Christ alone is the Head of the Church. The Covenanters took a stand for freedom and righteousness and the cost was high, many paying for their stand with their lives.

The first meeting of *Covenant Men* was on October 7, 1995 and 300 men from the Scottish Elim Churches met at Stirling Castle and from there they marched down to Stirling city centre to hold an open air service. This was followed by an inauguration service in The Church of the Holy Rude, situated close to Stirling Castle, a place steeped in Scottish history and with the graves of many Covenanters within its grounds. It's now more than twenty years on from that meeting in Stirling and the need for men who will covenant with God is greater than ever.

Another new avenue of opportunity that blossomed in my early days back in the Scottish Region was a growing fellowship with the other Pentecostal Churches in Scotland. It started with meetings with Peter Cochrane, the Regional Superintendent of The Assemblies of God, Ian Ross from the Apostolic Churches and John Carr, representing the Independent Pentecostal Churches in Scotland. We met together regularly and discovered a united desire for God to do something fresh in our land of Scotland. After a lot of prayer and discussion Peter shared with us a vision / dream that had been in his heart for a long time. It was encapsulated in the word PLUS – Pentecostals Linked and United for Scotland and from this was birthed the *PLUS* Gathering in Scotland.

We booked Butlin's at Ayr and had a difficult start as we took over the camp after an adult weekend. The place reeked of alcohol and had a lot of very hung-over revellers still on site to help 'welcome' 2000 Scottish Pentecostals who had booked to attend. The carpets in the main venues were sodden with alcohol and anyone falling down when prayed for ran the risk of getting up inebriated by another kind of spirit. Despite the messy start the Scottish Pentecostals had a powerful week of fellowship devoid of all denominational distinctives and enjoyed ministry from Bob Gordon and David Shearman. Those of us who had planned the event and booked the venue felt very grateful to God for this new breakthrough in Pentecostal unity.

As we continued to meet, talk and pray the idea for a combined training venue was birthed. Jim Gibson, who led the Cumbernauld Community Church, had recently bought an amazing building in Cumbernauld which became the home for the *PLUS* Training College. Callum Henderson, who up until then had led the South Gyle Elim Church, took charge and headed up a team of teachers who helped train men and women for ministry in Scotland.

Paul Scanlon was a guest speaker at one of the *PLUS* Gatherings at Ayr and his visit to Scotland led to a number of ministry trips by Margery and I to the Abundant Life Church in Bradford. We were blessed and challenged by the quality of the church we found there. There was a depth of maturity and commitment that was outstanding, everything they did had the stamp of quality on it and there was a freshness and exciting variety in all their outreach attempts to reach their city. This developing relationship with Abundant Life led to an invitation for Margery and I to become part of the team and so at the start of a new millennium we moved to Bradford.

It was only to be a short stay but a very important one for us. At this time I was a member of the Elim Executive (now the National Leadership Team) and also on a large number of committees. All of this contributed to a life that was increasingly controlled by committees and less and less involved with people. Going to Bradford involved resigning from the Executive Council and all Elim Committees and changing from being an Elim Alliance Minister to an Elim Church Incorporated minister. It was a massive change and from being at the centre of so much that was happening in Elim I was now very much out on the boundaries of Elim activity.

My role in Bradford was primarily pastoral but I was also involved in preaching in the public services and participation in their newly commenced Training School. From being in a fellowship like Elim where I was known by many, I moved to a church where I had no history and acceptance was earned by current input not historical connection. It was a massive challenge to confidence in my identity and my security in Christ; a hard lesson but, at that season in my life, a very important one for me to go through and a major disturbance of my comfort zone.

We are warned from Hebrews to expect shakings that will test our security and an intensifying of this as the end approaches – *'...but now he has promised, "Once more I will shake, not only the earth but also the heavens." The words "once more" indicate the removing of what can be shaken – that is created things – so that what cannot be shaken may remain,'* (Hebrews 12: 26, 27).

The danger for church in the West is that we have had it easy for so long, however, there are signs now that this is changing and while at the present the threat may only be prosecution but it will soon become persecution. The cost of being an authentic follower of Christ is rising and we see the emerging of the warnings of Jesus in Matthew 24 when He predicted that deception, wickedness and persecution would mean many abandoning the faith, many being deceived and the love of most growing cold (Matthew 24: 9-13). Sobering words that should be taken seriously and used to strengthen the dependable foundations of our walk with God.

Our short but very important time in Bradford came to an end by an invitation to take over from John Glass the leadership of the Kilsyth Church of God as he moved to Cheltenham to become Elim's new General Superintendent.

Following John was becoming a habit and replacing him in Kilsyth was a daunting challenge. Kilsyth was a church with a serious history in revival and John was its first full time leader in its distinguished history. But for me it was like returning to my roots as this church had played a big part in my formative years. Joe Gray, my first Bible Class leader and a man who had a profound effect on my life, was one of Kilsyth's leaders but sadly God had called him home before I returned. Joe was a builder by trade and Margery and I ended up buying the last home he built before he died. We had lived in many homes since our marriage but this one had a special place in our hearts and as an added bonus his widow, May Gray, lived opposite us.

Our move to Kilsyth was the unwrapping of one of the last chocolates in almost fifty years of ministry and it would contain for us the darkest experience of our lives but Kilsyth proved to be the very best possible place for us to go through it.

My Chocolate Box Journey

7

Through the Valley of the Shadow

It was at the beginning of a new millennium that Margery and I took over the leadership of the Kilsyth Church of God. The town of Kilsyth, nestling at the foot of the Kilsyth Hills and mid-way between Stirling and Glasgow, is not a large town, population 10,100 (2004) but a town with a unique history.

Most towns or cities have never experienced one revival but Kilsyth has experienced three. In 1742, after a series of devastating disasters, with the people of the town on the verge of starvation, God responded to the cry of desperate people and under the preaching of the parish minister, James Robe, the town was impacted by a visitation from God and hundreds of men and women cried out to God for mercy.

Then in 1839, when the spiritual condition of the town was in serious decline, the son of the parish minister preached on a number of occasions with remarkable results. William Chalmers Burns was assistant to Robert Murray McCheyne in Dundee and on one occasion, at an open air meeting near the Parish Church in Kilsyth, he preached to a crowd of 10,000 people. It was not unusual for hundreds of people to meet in the market square before going to work.

In 1896 an evangelistic association was started by the local parish ministers in a bid to make contact with the families of the mining community. Meetings were started in the Westport Hall and the church grew rapidly, then in 1908 the church experienced an outpouring of the Holy Spirit and Kilsyth became the centre for the Pentecostal Revival in Scotland. The Westport Hall became the home for this new and fresh move of God but in 1961 the building was destroyed by a fire and in 1962 the existing building was opened, having been erected totally by the labour of the local congregation.

(I am indebted to the research of James Hutchinson for a lot of this information.)

It was to a church with this heritage that Margery and I came in 2000. Although we had been in ministry for over thirty-five years this was our first church back home in Scotland. We had the advantage of a certain familiarity with the church and its background due to Kilsyth's involvement in the establishing of our home church at Motherwell. Also, Margery's father had been a miner as was also my grandfather so we knew something of the culture of a mining community. John Glass, my predecessor, during his time of leadership, had steered the church through a period of transition and change of thinking and practice so I came in with the additional advantage of his years of work.

Our commencement at Kilsyth almost got off to a bad start. New Year, referred to as Hogmanay, is always a big event in Scotland. Our memory of a typical Hogmanay meeting was that after bringing in the New Year it was time for fun, with people engaging in all sorts of items including singing, humorous skits etc. Margery and I decided that we would prepare something that would enter into the spirit of the occasion.

The song from 'Bob the Builder' was chosen with some new words we put to it and we got ourselves suitably dressed down with hard hats and stood ready in the corridor to be 'announced' by the convenor. Something made me peep into the hall to see what was happening before our contribution and to my horror I realised that things had changed in our decades of absence 'down south'. Instead of fun items, it was serious testimonies, spiritual songs or encouraging words for the year ahead. There followed a very quick change of clothes to become a sedate pastor and his wife and Bob the Builder was dumped for something more suitable. We can only imagine the shock/surprise there would have been if, following our introduction by the convenor, the new pastor and his wife had burst onto the stage dressed as builders singing a 'Bob the Builder' song!

The people of Kilsyth Church of God love fun so I think they would have laughed their heads off at our 'Bob the Builder' impersonation, but as well as fun they are very strongly motivated to involvement in God's work and when they start something it usually will not fail for lack of support. They have a culture of commitment that I have seldom seen equalled anywhere else. But there was another quality from many of the choice people of Kilsyth that was going to emerge and would prove to be of great support to Margery and me, a support that we would certainly need in great measure.

Life back in pastoral ministry was challenging and as time went on we discovered that the church had a very big heart for mission work, local, UK and overseas. The church developed a strong link with Teen Challenge and regularly had the lads from Whitchester House with us for the Sunday evening service. Regular fundraising events were organised and after one such event the church was able to present to John Macey (leader of Teen Challenge at that time) a cheque for £10,000.

On another occasion when I came back from a trip to the Philippines I reported on the dire conditions I had found in a local prison with cell overcrowding and no exercise or shower facilities for the prisoners. It was not long until the church started raising money and enough was sent for the local church in the Philippines to initiate building work to supply outdoor exercise facilities and showers. The local church also had enough to lay on a banquet for the prisoners and warders and Mark Ritchie, the Missionary, who was originally from Fraserburgh in North East Scotland, was able to preach the gospel to all assembled. The church could be wonderfully innovative in finding ways to raise money for missions. One young man even submitted to having his chest waxed, in public – 'Ouch!' That is giving till it hurts.

Kilsyth has an amazing number of very big hearted people and we were about to experience another evidence of this big hearted love.

It was at 7:40am on the morning of Tuesday February 7, 1998 that I got a phone call from Margery and it brought a dramatic change to our lives. Our daughter, Lorraine, had not long returned from Bangladesh where she had been working with VSO (Voluntary Service Overseas) helping to train nurses (Lorraine, like her mother Margery, was a nurse). Lorraine had cut short her tour of duty in Bangladesh and returned home unexpectedly. We were shocked at her emaciated condition when we met her off the train at Motherwell station. She was examined by a doctor who said she was suffering from an e-coli type infection but with lots of care and prayer, good medical support and home-cooked food she soon began to recover and finally declared she was ready to go back to Bristol to take up her nursing career again.

It wasn't too long, however, before Margery was called to go down to Bristol to once again care for Lorraine. It was during this visit that Margery discovered the real truth about Lorraine's condition, she was a heroin addict. This brings me back to the previously mentioned phone call that I received from Margery at 7:40am. Following the call I quickly made arrangements to go down to Bristol to join Margery and the rest of the family who, at that time, were all in the Bristol area. It took time for the whole story to unfold.

Our children were not sheltered from the dangers of drug addiction because in our days of leading the New Life Fellowship in Bristol we had *Life For The World*, a drug rehabilitation ministry, worshipping with us, our family were all involved in supporting the ministry and the lads who were in the programme, so they were well aware of the dangers of addiction. I remember standing in Lorraine's apartment, after we found out about her addiction and thinking that by God's grace and power we would soon see this heroin addiction broken and Lorraine completely set free. There are times when God delivers instantly but there are other times when He does not answer prayer in the way that we want. Our situation was to be the latter.

It took time for the whole story to emerge but we began to piece together what had happened. We wanted to know what had made Lorraine choose to resort to something as deadly as heroin. It began to unfold that Lorraine, when she was in Bangladesh, had gone down to Dhaka, the capital city, for a few days break. She had never found working in Bangladesh easy, especially when up in rural areas, because of the disrespectful attitude of many Bangladesh men to white women. While in Dhaka she had lost her purse and went to a police station to report the theft. While in the police station she was raped by four of the policemen, one of whom was the officer in charge. To add to the trauma of what had been done to her they threatened her that they would see to it that, if she told anyone, she would never get out of Bangladesh.

To help cope with the trauma of what had happened to her and with the added pressure of being unable to speak to anyone, Lorraine made the biggest mistake of her life and resorted to the very easy to obtain help of heroin which when taken can make the person feel detached (albeit temporarily) from life's problems. It had quickly become her way of coping with the devastating trauma of rape, and with the emergence of the awful truth so began the battle of our lives to help Lorraine through to freedom. As I said earlier, I was confident that we would quickly see this battle won. The whole family rallied to the task of supporting Lorraine and there were seasons when she was free from the addiction but we soon began to recognise the signs that the addiction was back. Margery gave herself unreservedly to care for our daughter, living with her for long stretches, even sleeping across the door to stop Lorraine slipping out to get heroin and going with her every day to the gym to keep her occupied and active.

The following is an excerpt from Lorraine's story.

Lorraine's own account of her battle with heroin

It's really hard to believe that I am about to write an account of the last six years of my life in which I will talk about violence, crime and drugs and that it is my life and experience I am talking about. I can remember reading about people involved in all of the above but it seemed so far removed from my life and experience that I would have laughed at anyone who would dare to have suggested that I would go down that road.

I was brought up in a fantastic, caring Christian home and can honestly say I have no bad memories of my childhood apart from the odd chastisement for naughty childish pranks and mischievousness. I always knew I was loved and so found it easy to love and respect others. I knew right from wrong and was never short of guidance. I wanted to be a nurse for as long as I can remember, my Mum's a nurse so I'm sure the inspiration for my chosen profession stemmed from her. I qualified as a nurse and found great pleasure (most of the time) in my work; I had some fantastic friends, a pretty good social life and I was happy.

I left Bristol, where I had trained and worked, to go travelling with friends through Asia and Australia. We had lots of fun without really a care in the world and so on coming home I knew I wanted to travel again but this time with a purpose. I had always had a desire to work in a developing country to (cheesy as it sounds) help people less fortunate than myself. I applied to VSO (Voluntary Service Overseas), was accepted and offered a job on a project in Bangladesh. I agreed to go and left in July 1996 to work there for two years.

While in Bangladesh I met some truly lovely people who were working in the poorest conditions with little or no supplies. At times I found the different culture very hard but I was determined to stay and achieve some of the things I had set out to do. Towards the end of my first year I was attacked by four policemen and went through a horrific experience. I had never ever really had anything bad happen to me before and was left very hurt, scared and completely unable to cope. I won't go into any more detail about what happened because I am only now dealing with it without the blocking factor of drugs. Heroin became my comforter following the attack, it is readily available in Bangladesh and, I have since discovered, just about anywhere.

I left Bangladesh and travelled back to my parents in Scotland completely addicted to heroin. It was of course not long before my family and close friends knew that something was very wrong.

The next few years were hell for everyone involved. I had become quite reclusive back in Bristol where I had moved back to live in a little bed-sit. Heroin for me was never a social thing; it was something I did secretly and on my own away from the world that I no longer wanted to be part of. I soon ran up large bills on my credit card and sold whatever I could to finance my now £100 a day habit. My friends and parents, once they knew, all wanted to help and tried everything but until the last year or so I really didn't want the help because, although I despised what I was doing and the hurt I was causing, I just could not turn my back, for very long anyway, on the thing that had become my memory suppressant and my comforter. With heroin in my system I felt OK and able to cope but without it I was a mess or so I thought at that time.

I did half-heartedly try to 'cold turkey' on numerous occasions because I knew that I just could not go on destroying my life and causing such pain to the ones around me, but the guilt I felt from my experience in Bangladesh and the guilt I had accumulated from hurting my family and friends just added to the things I wanted to block out and the only way I knew how to do this was to have heroin in my veins.

As with most things the more you use something the more you need it and by now my habit had escalated beyond my finances but money or no money my body needed and craved for more and more heroin. I started shoplifting to get money and was of course quickly caught. I tried it again and was again caught and had to go to Court. The humiliation of standing in that dock with my parents present is something I will never forget and seeing them with tears in their eyes nearly broke my heart – yet I still wanted more heroin and despised myself even more for needing it and wanting it.

To cut a long story short I ended up moving from the home of my parents in Scotland to Norwich to get help from a Christian organisation there. They generously took me in and allowed me to work for my keep whilst trying to help me stay clear of drugs. I was not an easy guest and often left to search for what had become my solace – heroin. They were very forgiving and always took me back. A change did begin to happen to me there, I began to slowly realise that there was a good life away from heroin and maybe, just maybe, I could work towards it. Throughout all my time addicted to heroin I despised yet loved it and by this stage I hated the fact that I needed it just to be able to get up and feel normal; the highs had long gone but I was one of the lucky ones because I knew that there was a good life out there away from drugs. Getting to it was the problem.

At this time I made a very special friend who gave me that added inspiration to sort my life out and so I eventually began to fight my addiction and with the help of some amazing people at the Bure Centre in Norwich, my family and friends I started to get free of heroin. It has been the fight of my life and I still have many battles to win because it is a daily struggle but I've been so lucky that I have the support of my family and friends and have been given sanctuary in the form of a home where I feel safe and accepted by two people I hardly knew but who have become special friends. They have allowed me to stay with them for almost a year and have coped with me overdosing, detoxing and being depressed. Without them or my other supports I would not be where I am today. I am just so grateful to them all.

The crime I committed last year in Kilsyth was to me my all-time low. It was this that really brought me to my knees and made me seek help from the Bure Drug Centre. I had gone to stay with my parents for yet another attempt at 'cold-turkey' but by day ten I was at my wits end and had awful cravings, which I didn't want to have and despised myself that I still did have; I just came to the conclusion that I would rather be dead than live this way, causing so much pain to those around me. I decided, in what I thought was a very rational way, that I needed to kill myself and the only way I knew I would be able to go through with it would be to overdose on heroin and to get this heroin I needed money.

Without thinking of the consequences for the poor lady I robbed I decided to go to the local store and demand money, thinking it would be all so easy. It wasn't, as the lady shopkeeper fought with me and after a struggle, in which I unintentionally hurt her, I escaped with some money, took my Dad's car and Mum's purse and headed to Glasgow where I purchased enough bags of heroin to hopefully kill myself.

I spoke on the phone to a close friend to say goodbye and apologise for what I was doing but I honestly thought everyone would be better off without me around. I did not realise that my friend was also on the phone to my Dad and they worked out where I was and my Dad arrived just in time to stop me finishing myself – something I am so grateful for now but not so much at the time.

I am now facing the consequences of those dreadful actions and will readily accept any punishment but it could not match what I have already put myself through. The horror and revulsion I feel because I could do such things will always stay with me and I am really struggling to forgive myself. However, with the help I have received and the fact that I am now fighting to recover I have now been clean for eight months and I am learning to once again enjoy the everyday pleasures of life and have fun again.

If one good thing could come out of all this misery I would be glad. If I could stop one person from making the same mistakes I have made I would be thrilled. What started as a comforter became my hell. Heroin is not a drug you can dabble with or use socially. There is nothing 'fun', clever or sociable about heroin addiction and as it did in my life it strips you of all morals, decency and self-respect; it is all-consuming, full-time and a greedy companion that very quickly consumes every bit of your life and will, if allowed, destroy anyone close to it.

I now hate what I once loved and would beg anyone not to be duped into using it by the sometimes-tempting package it can come wrapped in or by the things it can promise to do for you. Heroin addiction is not fun or glamorous. Unfortunately, it is readily available on our streets and what may start as a bit of fun or an answer to a problem will remain as neither. There is no fun in having to live a deceitful and criminal life-style and what may seem as the answer to a problem brings with it a whole new set of problems which will make the original problem pale into insignificance.

There is help available. I have been amazed at the support I have been given and will forever be grateful for that and for the fact that the people close to me never quite gave up on me. I am now at last a recovering addict and if I can do it so can others. I hope my story will help others to realise that there is hope and help available for those that really want it. There is life after heroin addiction.

Post Script

On November 22, 2004, Lorraine died from a heroin overdose. After a considerable period free from addiction Lorraine started using again, just a little at first, but then in increasing amounts. She had been very happy in a good job in a call centre and was doing very well but then due to cash problems beyond the control of the company they had to close and Lorraine was made redundant. Because of her police record good jobs were hard to come by but she finally got a job labouring on a building site. While she was glad for the employment and had good camaraderie with the men on the site, it did not present her with the challenge that she so needed. It appears that a sense of despair began to slowly set in and a feeling that life was not really going to change and to help cope with these emotions she reverted back to heroin, an occasional 'treat' at first but then the addiction really began to kick in and this time there just was not the motivation to continue the fight. Her mother and I at first were unaware of this but began to detect some of the tell-tale signs and our fears were finally confirmed.

Lorraine was willing to go to Teen Challenge, which is a Christian rehabilitation centre in South Wales. The first time she went in she only lasted a few days before the overpowering desire for heroin made her leave and head for the streets of Swansea to find a dealer. She did return to Norwich and eventually was once again willing to go back to Teen Challenge but the outcome was the same as before – leaving after a few days in the centre to get back to the streets of Swansea to locate the always 'easy-to-find' dealers. Again she made her way back to Norwich and it was there on the morning of November 23 that her body was discovered in a car in Norwich. We don't believe that the dose was taken with the intention of killing herself but her body was by now very weakened by drug misuse and what before could be taken without serious effect this time proved fatal.

Lorraine's funeral service at Proclaimers International in Drayton, Norwich, was an amazing event. People came from all over the country and as well as family, friends from nursing days, backpacking days, childhood days and more recent times, the building was full. Her brother Andrew gave a very moving tribute in the form of an open letter to his sister and as well as highlighting her many beautiful characteristics gave everyone an insight into some of the mischief the two of them got up to in childhood. There was hardly a dry eye in the building. More tributes and insights were paid by those who had been close to Lorraine in her Norwich days. *'She wanted to make a difference'* was the theme that kept recurring through them all.

Margery and I miss her terribly but the many wonderful memories from childhood through to the present is a consolation. Even in the difficult years of addiction the real

Lorraine kept breaking through and she had an amazing ability to make everyone laugh, she could light up a room and mix so easily with anyone who was in that room. She has left a lasting legacy of happiness in all the lives she touched. She did make a difference.

In the midst of this trauma I still had the responsibility for the church in Kilsyth but discovered the amazing support they gave Margery and I through it all. With several court appearances the newspapers inevitably got hold of the story and this meant some very unwelcome publicity but the leaders and members of the church were like a solid wall of support around us. Margery and I will never forget the love and support we got from our Church of God family.

Little did we realise that another storm of darkness was about to engulf us.

8

More Testing

As Margery and I were struggling to recover from the sad end to Lorraine's seven year struggle, a lot of other things were also happening in our lives. I had been diagnosed with severe glaucoma in both eyes and eventually had to surrender my driving licence. I would never have believed how big a life-changer losing your licence could be. Life with a car has a lot of freedom and flexibility but life without being able to drive needs a lot more planning and foresight. Fortunately Margery could drive but disliked it intensely. I had to work very hard at being a good passenger who kept his opinions to himself. You will need to ask Margery just how successful I was at it, but it was not easy for either of us. There was also the looming prospect of retirement which seemed to have sneakily crept up on me, I did not feel ready to face it but other events were going to take a hand in that decision.

Meanwhile, our daughter Yvonne was having a battle with her own health issues; the death of her sister had hit her very hard. This meant that Margery was needed more frequently down in Bristol to give some additional care to Yvonne who had a young son, Joseph, to look after. Also, our son, Andrew and his family had emigrated to Australia shortly before Lorraine's death so we were feeling their loss on top of all the other challenges we faced.

Yvonne's health had never been robust and she struggled with a number of issues that weakened her. Her husband, Andy, organised a holiday to Gran Canaria to try and help her general condition. While in Gran Canaria she had a fall and broke her leg. During the operation to reset the leg she unfortunately ingested some vomit and developed Bacterial Pneumonia and was seriously ill. As quickly as flights allowed Margery and I got to Gran Canaria to be with Andy and Joseph and at Yvonne's bedside.

The medics did all they could and there was a huge prayer initiative for her recovery but despite it all she did not recover after her operation and died in the hospital. It was a very sad journey home. It is hard to describe our feelings at that time; for myself, I felt I had to lay aside my own emotions to be of help to Margery who was going through emotional pain that only mothers will understand. My time for grieving would come later. Margery has an amazing and consistent trust in God and her personal faith in the ways and plans of God would eventually see her through this dreadful storm. Another sad funeral followed with our friend, John Glass, once again being asked to give the message. It required someone of John's experience and ability to handle this kind of situation – the death of two daughters within eighteen months, and he did it with compassion and insight. John had been a close friend to our children in our days together in Bristol but has also been a friend of ours for many years so, despite the pain to him, he was the right choice to lead the service.

Once again the members of Kilsyth Church of God were there for us; the emotional support, the practical care, the amazing financial generosity, the prayers and the words of comfort – together provided an amazing blanket of support to surround us. Many of them had been through dark valleys themselves so ministered to us out of their own developed trust in God through their difficult times. What an amazing church to be in as we faced the biggest challenges of our lives.

With all that had happened, and the fact that I was now 65, it was time to seriously consider retirement. Kilsyth now needed a new leader and we needed to relocate to Bristol so that we could be of support and help to Andy, our son-in-law, and Joseph our grandson who was only five and missing his mother. The house was put on the market and the date for the farewell service was fixed. It actually turned out to be two services with Saturday being an opportunity for other churches from the town to be present. Kilsyth may be a town of only 10,000 people but it has several very strong churches and the ministers had all played a big part in our support. I spoke at the Sunday morning service and afterwards the whole church had lunch together which was the unhurried opportunity to say goodbye to people we had grown very close to in our years in Kilsyth.

We decided it would be a good idea to visit our son in Australia before the move south, being with Andrew and his wife and the grandchildren would be good therapy after all we had been through and the thought of lots of sunshine was so attractive. We eventually got a buyer for the house but with the problem that they wanted access when we would still be in Australia. We agreed to the sale and arranged for the house to be emptied as we left for our trip to the other side of the world and all our furniture put in store with Pickfords, the removal company. The new owner would get the key from the solicitor when the sale was complete.

It all seemed to be coming together so perfectly. The holiday in Australia was just what the doctor ordered, lovely sunshine, grandchildren to enjoy, new places to visit, lots of outdoor eating and swimming in the pool. We began to feel the benefits of it all and felt ready to go home and undertake the move to the Bristol area. Then we got a phone call from the buyer of our house to say that her buyer had pulled out and she would need to do the same.

We always commit these decisions to God but wondered how this was going to work out in practice. We contacted Pickfords, the removal company, and asked them to return all our furniture only to discover that they had shipped it all down to Bristol to await our arrival there. They agreed to bring it all back north in time for our return (at their expense). On our journey home we changed planes at Singapore and while there we got a phone call from a friend, Callum Henderson, to say that he and his wife, Izzy, wanted to buy our house but only when they had sold theirs. So we got a buyer for our house while sitting in Changi Airport in Singapore which gave some hope as we continued our journey to Scotland. We then had the strange task of unpacking our much travelled furniture, which we had packed up just a few weeks earlier. There then followed the most problematic move we have ever encountered in our lives, it took one year and during that time we moved a total of five times. When we finally got the keys of our new home our friend, Pete Standerwick, gave our house a name – 'At Last'.

We had chosen Yate as our desired place to live, it wasn't too far from Andy and Joseph and the property prices were affordable. There was also a good Elim Church within one hundred yards of our home, Gateway Revival Church, pastored by Paul and Miriam James; Paul had been a student under me during my time in the Bible College. Paul and the church gave us a very warm welcome and I was given plenty of opportunity to minister in the fellowship which I found so helpful at a time when so many other things were being taken from my life.

Gateway continues to be our spiritual home, Paul and Miriam have moved on to lead a church in London but with the rest of the church we are now eagerly awaiting the arrival of our new leaders, Marty and Rebekah who will shortly leave the Amazon where they have been missionaries for twelve years.

My *Chocolate Box Journey* has now taken on a different flavour due to the onset of Parkinson's disease. The symptoms, while not restricting normal life too much, have necessitated me giving up preaching and most public ministry. I have not found this easy. As I mentioned near the beginning, one of my favourite characters in the New Testament is Philip, referred to as Philip the Evangelist; I think I have preached on him more than anyone else in the Bible (apart from the Lord). I have loved following his journey from new convert in the Jerusalem Church, then serving as a carer for the church widows followed by a new venture in evangelism after the scattering of the church due to persecution. His ministry in Samaria saw revival hit the city and that was followed by a sudden transfer from the revival in Samaria to a lonely encounter in the desert with the Ethiopian Chancellor of the Exchequer. Then after supernatural transportation from the desert he found himself in Azotus and preached the gospel in surrounding villages ending up in Caesarea.

More than twenty years later Paul and his companions arrive at Caesarea and Philip is still there, in fact the whole group stayed with Philip. I suspect that Philip met his wife in Caesarea and settled there, they had four daughters. The point I want to make is that Philip, after a varied journey serving God in some very exciting situations, then came to a time in life that was more settled and less dramatic – but he was still serving God and his home was a place of ministry to the man who was now spearheading the advance of the Gospel, the Apostle Paul. My journey has been varied, exciting, challenging and difficult plus a few more descriptive words but my desire in this new season is to, like Philip, still be serving in whatever way I now can.

Once, when I was reading through the Gospel of Mark, I was struck by the number of times Mark drew attention to the response of people to the ministry of Jesus – *'everyone was amazed...they were filled with awe, the people were amazed at his teaching...they were so amazed, they were completely astonished, they were overwhelmed with amazement, overwhelmed with wonder, the disciples were astonished.'* Mark summed it up – *'He has done everything well'.*

We must never lose our capacity to be amazed by what Jesus does in our lives. My journey is a testimony to the amazing grace of God. That grace was at work even before I was born, it was powerfully experienced when I knelt on the ground with Duncan Campbell in a tent in Motherwell, it was joyfully received when grace provided me with a wonderful woman to be married to for fifty three years, God's grace gave us three wonderful children who brought us a lot of joy and that grace continues to this day, providing, protecting, correcting, forgiving and guiding. It's all about grace.

Some are born with so many blessings and abilities yet manage to squander the opportunity for a well-lived life while others may be gifted with far less but by God's grace and their determination they live a life that glorifies God and blesses many people. By birth Jacob seemed to have a lot less than his brother and lived under the shadow of his popular, athletic and macho brother. His mother didn't help him much either and by her influence and input into his life helped shape him into a very clever manipulator. But of course Jacob made his own choices and by his devious ways managed to cause a furious family split between himself and his father-in-law. But then one day, when Jacob was facing an encounter with his very angry brother who was coming to meet him accompanied by four hundred men, he had a life-changing meeting with God. The story of this amazing encounter is found in Genesis 32 and is, to me, one of the most astonishing stories in the Bible when God took on human form to have a wrestling match with a rogue and a twister. At the end, Jacob limped away with a permanent injury to remind him of the day he struggled with God and pressed through into the blessing of a new life as Israel not Jacob.

It's amazing what God can do with a Jacob or a James for that matter. As well as the wonderful variety of opportunities God has given us I am also amazed at the international opportunities in missions God has opened for Margery and I. It was in 1986 that we made our first missions trip to South Africa representing Elim Missions at some denominational conferences and visiting our missionaries in Zimbabwe and Tanzania. Since then opportunities have opened for us to visit other African countries like Rwanda, Kenya, Botswana and Swaziland as well as Brazil, Ukraine, America, Hong Kong, Thailand, Italy, Israel, France and Belgium.

When I think of our beginnings in Scotland, the difficulties of upbringing in families that struggled to make ends meet, very ordinary educations etc I can only marvel at what God can do with lives that are given over to Him. What enriching opportunities we have had as we met and ministered with some of the finest missionaries and overseas workers you could ever meet. Names that, sadly few would now know – Peter and Brenda Griffiths, Alan and Anne Renshaw, Joy Bath, Freda Grossen and many others. Our lives were blessed as we saw, first hand, the level of their sacrifice and commitment.

I am coming to end of this record of my journey thus far. Thank you for continuing to this point. I hope that in some way my story has helped and given you courage to continue on your journey. I am sure you are aware that the word 'Gospel' means 'good news' but it can also mean 'good story'. The gospel is the greatest story ever told and when that gospel comes to a life it produces the greatest story in that life. Rejoice in your story of God's grace at work in your life and never lose the joy of sharing your story with others. We are all writing a story, the story of our life, and by God's grace and activity in our lives every one can be a classic.

In the next and last chapter I have recorded some reflections as I look back over the lessons learned on this journey into grace. Margery and I have learned lessons about ourselves, the importance of dependable friends who will brave storms with you but above all the certainty of God's abiding and continuing presence and power that is always at work, even in the times when He seemed far away. God blessed the latter end of Job's life more than the first and we continue our journey in the same expectation, knowing that we worship the same God as Job.

Reflections

From my earliest days I have fully accepted, without reservation, the whole Bible as the inspired Word of God. There are some verses that you believe, but you have to wait a long time to fully appreciate and experience their meaning. Psalm 37:25 is one such verse – *'I have been young but now I am old yet I have never seen the righteous forsaken or their children begging bread.'*

I have always believed this verse but have now experienced it. The righteous are not protected from the pressures and problems of life but they have the assurance that in everything God is working for the good of those who love Him and are called according to His purposes. Retirement is an opportunity to reflect on life and its lessons and Solomon, the writer of Proverbs, took a lot of time to pass on to his children the wisdom that he had gained from his journey. My prayer is that as you read this book there may be some wisdom in it that will help you on your journey.

The journey

As mentioned previously, in my childhood my family enjoyed an annual holiday at Rothesay, on the Island of Bute, which is off the West Coast of Scotland. For me the holiday did not begin when we got to Rothesay, the adventure started the moment we left home. First it was the train to Glasgow and in those days it was steam trains and the thrill of sticking your head out of the window and being immersed in steam was part of the fun. Then it was boat from Wemyss Bay or Gourock to Rothesay. There was a variety of boats that made the crossing but often it would be *The Waverley*, a paddle steamer that is still taking people on holiday excursions.

Once the boat left the pier my father would take me down to see the engines and being an engineer he would give me a great description of how they worked. Once the engine room visit was over it was straight to the dining area for a snack, usually a Scottish mince pie and a bottle of Irn Bru, a favourite Scottish soft drink. Then it was up to the front of the boat to get blown to bits by the wind and have a running commentary of all the places of interest that we passed en route to our holiday island.

The journey itself was a big part of the overall experience. For followers of Christ, heaven is our final destination and what pleasures await us there but the journey to get there is also part of the thrill. I have enjoyed my journey thus far and determine to continue to do so until I reach the final destination. Can I encourage you to enjoy your journey? There is so much to enjoy on our pilgrimage so don't be so concentrated on the final destination that you miss the places and people of interest that we can encounter on the way.

Light beyond the darkness

*'The people remained at a distance while Moses approached the thick darkness **where God was**,'* (Exodus 20:21).

What an astonishing place to find God – in the darkness. And it wasn't just ordinary darkness – it was thick darkness, but beyond that darkness was a light so brilliant that when Moses finally emerged his face shone with the glory of God. The people remained at a distance but Moses not only approached the thick darkness he pressed through it and found the light beyond the darkness.

There are experiences in our following of the Lord that can be dark and for some it is thick darkness, when the temptation can be to *'remain at a distance'*. Darkness can be frightening but for the courageous and the persistent there can be light beyond the darkness.

In Mark 10 we find the disciples going through a similar experience on their journey of following Jesus. They had followed Him through the season of popularity when they had been amazed by the miracles, signs and wonders, and had witnessed remarkable things, even to the dead being raised. But the tone of the journey now changed. They had seen the glory of God in the face of Jesus but now they saw another look on His face that frightened them; it was set like flint and He was heading for Jerusalem with a fixed determination − *'they were on their way up to Jerusalem with Jesus leading the way and* **the disciples were astonished while those who followed were afraid,'** (Mark 10:32).

They continued to follow but it all seemed different now. This was not what they had expected when they committed to follow Christ and they hadn't read this in the small print either. The journey of walking with the Lord will inevitably challenge us to progress from the superficial to the serious, from the virtually real to the real. Our willingness to follow the Good Shepherd will sometimes take us through *'the valley of the shadow'* and there we will meet the *'rod and the staff'*. Few want to venture into this challenging realm, the green pastures and quiet waters can seem much more attractive.

When our daughter Yvonne was lying critically ill with bacterial pneumonia in a Gran Canaria hospital there was a massive prayer initiative across the country and further afield, yet despite this she finally died. This, on top of the death of Lorraine only months earlier, left Margery and I in a state of shock and grief. I felt I was struggling, unsuccessfully, to make sense of what God was doing or even where God was in all of it. Like David after Uzzah's death I was angry at what had happened but, also like David, I felt a tremble of fear as I realised my exceeding smallness in the face of the awesomeness of God and His 'beyond-our-understanding' ways. God is not simple, nor are His long-term plans and, He seldom explains Himself (He doesn't have to). So often like those first disciples fearfully following Christ on His last journey to Jerusalem we loved it when Christ was drawing the crowds but slow the pace when the going (and the understanding) gets tough.

In John 6 we have what I call 'the watershed sermon' – it started out brilliantly with everyone hanging on Jesus' words and eager to do what He wanted but by the end of the sermon the crowds melted away and only twelve were left. We revel in the high moments of emotional drama when the crowds are singing His praise and wanting to make Him King but feel the temptation to walk away when what He is saying or doing dramatically disturbs our comfort zone. This is clearly illustrated in the difference in attendance between a gathering featuring a popular singer and an exciting 'man of the moment' preacher; compared to a meeting focussing on a speaker with a call to repent and change and a serious exposition of the life-affecting implications of truly following Christ. No contest. The numbers attending will speak for themselves.

The experience of Sinai was terrifying for the people and even for Moses the sight was so frightening that he said *'I am trembling with fear'*. For the Israelites the experience was unique, the only nation to hear the actual voice of God and see the glory of God in such an awesome way on a mountain that was quaking with the power of God's presence.

Yet despite this amazing experience and within a time frame of forty days they were dancing round an idol and proclaiming that a god of gold had brought them up out of Egypt. Can you believe that? The sad truth is that for many modern worshippers who have experienced the grace and goodness of God in amazing ways, yet still they walk away from the Lord when He has not come through in a way that they had expected Him to. Too many today can be just as fickle in their commitment to God as the Children of Israel were in the Sinai Desert.

David's experience of the fear of the Lord at Perez Uzzah, the disciples' encounter with fear as they followed Him on that journey to Jerusalem and Moses' fear in front of Sinai as he entered into the thick darkness where God was, all challenge us to press on in our journey with God even when the current experience is daunting and dark. For David there was eventually a glorious arrival for the Ark in Jerusalem, for Moses there was a shining face experience as he entered into the light beyond the darkness and for the disciples a glorious resurrection after the darkness of Calvary.

I remember Bob Gordon once quoting from CS Lewis' *The Lion, the Witch and the Wardrobe*. Lucy was asking about Aslan, the lion. 'Is he safe?' she asked. 'Safe?' said Mr Beaver, 'Don't you hear what Mrs Beaver tells you? Of course he's not safe…but he's good…he's the King.' Our God isn't safe but He's good. He's the King!

I mentioned at the start of the book that *'the fear of the Lord'* is the place to begin on the journey to acquire the wisdom we need to live life well. Isaiah 66:2 records an amazing statement from God where He describes the person that gets His attention – *'This is the one I esteem (place a high value on): he who is humble and contrite and who trembles at my word.'* God places a high value on the person who is attentive to what He says and who knows what it is to tremble at His word. This will necessarily take us into experiences with God that are beyond the nice and the comfortable, it will mean us launching out into deep waters and into 'beyond-our-understanding' experiences.

Maybe you feel a bit like David; you have embarked on a faith project which you were confident would glorify God and was in His will only to see it crumble in front of your eyes. This outcome may have left you confused, disillusioned and embarrassed and you are thinking: 'Lord why? What did I do wrong?' Or maybe like the disciples on that Jerusalem journey you are perplexed at the change of climate. The heady days of blessing, success and emotional highs seem a distant memory and you long for some light at the end of a very dark tunnel. You are learning new aspects of God's character and they leave you a bit scared. The process that God is willing for you to go through to bring you to a place of mature sonship can be daunting.

Question: 'How do you recognise a person of faith?' Is it the breadth of their glistening smile, or the bounce in their step as they take the platform or the mind boggling testimonies of powerful answers to prayer? Hebrews 11:39 can be hard to explain if your required evidence of faith is in visible answers and measurable success – *'these were all commended for their faith yet none of them received what had been promised. God had planned something better for us so that only together with us would they be made perfect'.* They did not receive what was promised, and probably eagerly hoped for, yet they were commended, by God no less, for their faith.

I would like to tell you about one of the most remarkable young ladies I ever met. Her name was Linda Meiklejohn, and she was married to Paul who at the time of this story pastored the Edinburgh Elim Church. Linda had a very infectious personality, happy, full of fun, mischievous but oh so real, down to earth and transparent. In her late thirties she embarked on a long held ambition and started training as a nurse. Not long after she qualified she was diagnosed with cancer and so began a hard journey with all the highs and lows that cancer sufferers are so familiar with.

She and Paul had massive and long-term support from their amazing church but despite a persistent and concerted prayer initiative she grew steadily worse. I visited Linda a number of times in the Edinburgh Hospice where she spent her last few weeks and found our conversations illuminating and challenging.

'Everyone praying for my healing as the most important thing,' she said one day, but she continued, 'the most important thing is not my physical healing but that I keep my faith intact.' Another time as she was close to death she said, 'I don't know how I would cope with healing now as I am so ready for heaven.' Linda, brought up in the Gorbals of Glasgow, had grasped the greatest wisdom of all. She had lived well and was ready to die well. Wesley said of his fellow Methodists, 'our people die well.' How you live will determine how you face the inevitable challenge of death. That is why people need to discover the right wisdom to know how to live their lives well and face death, not as a tragedy, but as a triumph crowning a life lived by God's wisdom.

When I pastored the Kilsyth Church of God we had in the church a young lady called Leslie Henderson. Leslie, like so many others, had to face the challenge of discovering she had breast cancer. One Sunday I asked her to give a testimony about how she was coping with this challenge. Something she said during her testimony has stuck with me – 'to receive a gift of healing is a wonderful miracle but not to receive a miracle of healing and yet continue to grow is more wonderful.' Now that's maturity!

Preachers are called upon to 'comfort the disturbed' but also to 'disturb the comfortable'. In Deuteronomy God is pictured as an eagle 'stirring up its nest', this is a vivid picture of the lengths to which an eagle will go to get her offspring out of the nest and flying. It can involve her lining the nest with thorns to make it less comfortable and could also mean her tearing the nest apart in her effort to get the eaglets to stretch their wings and do what they were created to do. So often God's people are like those young eagles – sitting comfortably in our often magnificent nests, complete with every conceivable aid and convenience to make church an 'exciting and enjoyable' experience, maybe the occasional squabble with fellow nest dwellers and also consuming great quantities of pre-digested food brought to us on a regular basis. We end up looking out of the nest, dreaming of flying and doing great exploits but never actually taking the risk to get out of the nest to do them.

If you are one of those looking forward to some peace and quiet in heaven then Revelation 19 will be a disappointment to you. It is a chapter full of shouting and noise and one of the causes for noisy celebration is that *'the wedding of the Lamb has come **and the Bride has made herself ready'**.* The Bride (the Church) prepared and ready to meet the Bridegroom (Christ). Now, not even the most faith filled and optimistic preacher could by any stretch of the imagination declare that the church (especially in the Western hemisphere) is ready to meet the Lord and dressed in the fine bright and clean linen which is the righteous acts of the saints. The church is not ready **but she will be** and God is stirring up the nest to get her out of her comfort zone experience to be what He intended her to be.

Margery and I were married in the Motherwell Elim Church on June 28th 1963. On the day of the wedding as I was in town to get a haircut, I turned a corner and ran straight into Margery. In those days it was considered very bad for the couple to see each other before the wedding ceremony. As we met face to face a look of horror came over Margery's face and without saying a word she turned and ran away from me up the street! The love of my life who was to become my wife in a few hours was running away from me! She had not yet been to the hairdresser, no makeup had been applied and she was wearing an everyday coat. She did not look like a bride but in a very short time, at 4pm, when the organ began to play and the doors were opened to allow her to enter – 'the bride had made herself ready!' and she was a picture.

Moses, David and the disciples that I have spoken about all went through a dark experience, it seemed as though God was absent but they came to realise that it was part of His preparation to move them on from the ordinary to the extraordinary, from the superficial to the sublime. Why should we think that it will be any different for us? We want glory on the cheap, breakthrough in three easy steps and at a time and place convenient to our timetable. But God wants to bring many full-grown sons to glory, not infants still craving milk as Hebrews 6 says – *'Let us leave the elementary, let us go on to maturity'*. Hebrews 6 also warns us about the danger of staying on milk when we should be onto meat.

Our daughter, Yvonne, was born at home and after the birth was over I cooked Margery a luscious steak with all the trimmings, at the same time I prepared a bottle of milk for Yvonne. Yvonne could not have handled a steak and Margery would not have been impressed with milk, which is for babies not grown adults. You've got the picture.

This process of preparation and maturity is not an easy one but God is more concerned about my character than my comfort whereas if I am honest I am more committed to my comfort.

Problem with prayer

Since my earliest years prayer has been a part of my life. In my pre-conversion years it was a ritual engaged in more out of fear of what would go wrong if I didn't say 'my prayers' before I went to sleep. After my conversion, however, it became a regular part of my daily spiritual disciplines. I have always been an early riser and believed that, for me, the best part of the day for reading and prayer was early morning before the routine of the day took over.

The events of the last few years have challenged my understanding of prayer more than at any time in my life. In the course of a two year period my oldest daughter died of bacterial pneumonia in a Gran Canaria hospital, my youngest daughter died of a heroin overdose after a long fight with her addiction, I had to surrender my driving licence because of glaucoma in both eyes, Margery lost her best friend to cancer, we had the most problematic house move of our entire lives, our son and his family emigrated to Australia and on top of all that I went through the major life change of retirement.

Alongside all of this I witnessed close friends also undergo huge life shaking traumas. All of these events, especially the loss of my two daughters, were faced with very large prayer initiatives but despite all the prayer there were no miracles. It seemed that when God was needed most He was totally absent. The silence of heaven was so painful. The One I had walked with all my life, had sought to serve, obey and honour was not a very present help in time of trouble. I felt hurt, angry, perplexed, abandoned and very confused. I went through a lot of heart searching; had I sinned, stepped out of the will of God or done something to make God so deaf to all my cries? It was a very testing time.

I have always enjoyed the writings of Philip Yancey, his thorough investigative and captivating style has always gripped me. But I feel he has excelled himself in his book called *Prayer*. In it he fully explores a difficult subject and is not afraid to deal with some of the major problems that many find with the subject. The events of the last few years have made me look again at prayer and as Yancey says in the subtitle, 'does it make any difference?'

The struggles of the last few years have made me examine a lot of things and I am slowly coming to new conclusions on prayer, I certainly feel that I for one have completely misunderstood its purpose. I knew a lot of things with my head but in my heart I looked on prayer as a 'hot-line' to heaven to get God to come in on my side and help me through a particular problem. I completely underestimated the opposition and the potential there is when a person on earth prays. No wonder Paul said *'we wrestle not against flesh and blood but against principalities and powers and spiritual wickedness in high places'*.

Revelation 5:8 and 8:3 have an important truth on prayer,

*'The four living creatures and the twenty four elders fell down before the Lamb. Each one had a harp and they were holding golden bowls full of incense which are **the prayers of the saints**,'* and *'Another angel who had a golden censer came and stood at the altar. He was given much incense to offer with **the prayers of all the saints**.'*

Our prayers, like our tears, are precious to God and have been collected in golden bowls so they can be poured out before Him like incense. It is (all) the prayers of all the saints, even the ones that did not receive the desired answer on earth – they are all precious to God.

I sat on a bus on one occasion and the lady beside me was reading a book, I was close enough to read the title, *How To Get Your Prayers Answered.* I was tempted to ask her if the book had a written guarantee with it, but I didn't. Prayer is more than just getting what we want or need from God; it is as much about me becoming aware of what God wants.

Jesus prayed a lot as He approached Calvary. He prayed for His disciples, He prayed for future disciples, He prayed for God's glory but His shortest and most powerful prayer was in the Garden of Gethsemane, it consisted of about twenty words. He prayed it three times and it concludes, *'Not my will, but yours be done'.* There is no greater prayer we can pray than for God's will to be done.

And Finally... The Greatest Story of All

I was born into a good family with a good heritage but in July of 1953 I was 'born again' into another family with an even greater heritage. The term 'born again' is used in the Bible to describe the Christian's conversion experience. My first family were all good people, my father was an elder in the church and my mother, brother and sister were all involved in South Dalziel Parish Church in Motherwell. But all of us, at different times, came to realise that our church involvement plus all our good works did not make us fit to stand before God.

When God made the world, His crowning act of creation was Adam and Eve, made in His own image to enjoy fellowship with Himself. But for them to be fully human God endowed them with the ability to choose, a wonderful but dangerous gift. They were given a simple test of this freewill in God's command not to partake of one of the trees in the wonderful garden they lived in. They exercised their ability to choose, but unfortunately they made a wrong one, they chose to disobey God. This choice had short and long-term consequences, it affected their relationship with God, with each other and with their environment. Their choice introduced into their lives and of all succeeding generations the negative and destructive elements that plague human life today; fear, hate, sickness, division, shame, blame, war, death etc. So often God gets the blame for what really is the consequence of our continuing rebellion against His Word and His ways.

But there is good news. Although God was the One sinned against He was the One who initiated a long-range plan to provide an answer to the rebellion, and the pain, of mankind. The plan began at the original moment when our fore-fathers made their disastrous choice to disobey and it reached its fulfilment at the birth of Jesus Christ, God's Son, into our world. Christ came to reveal to us the heart of God and His overwhelming desire for His creation to be reconciled.

The ultimate demonstration of God's love was the death of Christ on the Cross and by that death God has provided a way for every one who will put their faith in Christ to receive complete and total forgiveness for their sins. My mother and I made that choice in July of 1953 at some special meetings in a tent in Merry Street in Motherwell. Shortly after that my sister made her commitment to Christ at an evangelistic meeting in the Gaumont Cinema, again in Motherwell. My father, despite his religious pedigree, realised his need and made his decision before he died of cancer in the Belvidere Hospital in Glasgow. It was many years later that a friend from Africa, Sam Stark, helped my brother, Tom, realise his need of a Saviour.

No matter what direction your life-journey may have taken you on, the most important moment for any of us is our encounter with Christ; this alone determines our eternal welfare. I may never have met you but the fact you have read my book up to this point gives me great pleasure, so I finish with the most important question any one of us will ever face in life and it has to do with our relationship to Christ and the decision we need to make regarding God's offer of salvation through him.

As a lad of twelve God gave me the opportunity to make that life-changing decision and I have never regretted it for one moment, it positively shaped the rest of my life, right up to this moment sixty-three years later. I have come to know that God always wants what is good and best for my life and He wants exactly the same for you. His best plan and purpose for you is wrapped up in the gift of His Son, Jesus Christ. I can sum it up no better than these verses from the Bible, *'God so loved the world that he gave his one and only Son, that whoever believed in him shall not perish but have eternal life. For God did not send his Son into the world to condemn the world but to save the world through him,' (John 3:16-18).*

Other books by Jim Dick

Soul Food

A devotional book that takes the reader to some of the lesser known parts of the Bible to discover life-enhancing truths.

John Glass, Elim Church Former General Superintendent writes, *'The wisdom you are about to encounter has been forged on the anvil of reality and distilled in the crucible of faith. The soul-food that Jim places before you is "haute-cuisine" indeed – a banquet that is Biblically based and spiritually sound. This book is long overdue but like a good meal, eagerly anticipated, it will not disappoint.'*

Available in hard copy from Jim at *jimdick41@gmail.com*
£5 plus P&P
Also on Kindle from Amazon

The Success of the Secret Life

Based on *The Beatitudes* which are the introduction to the most famous sermon Jesus ever preached – 'The Sermon on the Mount'. Consisting of only 141 words which, even at a slow pace can be read in their entirety in a few minutes yet, despite their brevity, there is nothing in the whole of Scripture that compares with the sheer depth and challenge of these eight 'blessings' from the mouth of Jesus. They are foundational teaching for every follower of Christ. Straightforward and practical instruction that will introduce the reader to the essential attitudes and character of a disciple of Jesus.

Available on Kindle from Amazon

The Heroes of Baghdad

The Heroes of Baghdad delivers powerful and practical teaching for Christians living in a hostile culture. Followers of Christ are now described as 'the most persecuted religious body on the planet'. Jesus Himself warned us that persecution would reach a peak prior to His return. So it is not surprising that his most repeated challenge for us is for us to be ready and watchful. The backdrop to *The Heroes of Baghdad* is the lives of Daniel, Shadrach, Meshach and Abednego and the example they give us in knowing how to keep a consistent testimony but doing it in a way that makes the message of Christ attractive.

Available on Kindle from Amazon

Coming soon...

The Tale of Two Cities

Not Paris and London as in the novel by Charles Dickens but Jerusalem and Antioch from the Acts of the Apostles.

An exploration of the major flaw in Jerusalem which hindered it from fulfilling the Great Commission and the success factors in Antioch that made it a world-affecting church. Essential reading at a time when the role of modern church is being seriously scrutinised.